# A guide to the care and preservation of medieval cathedrals and churches

**General editor**: Colin Bassett BSc, FCIOB, FFB

*Other related titles*

Tree roots and buildings, *D. Cutler and I. B. K. Richardson*
Air and rain penetration of buildings, *P. Marsh*
Common building defects, *National Building Agency*
Remedial treatment of buildings, *B. A. Richardson*
Wood preservation, *B. A. Richardson*

# A GUIDE TO THE CARE AND PRESERVATION OF MEDIEVAL CATHEDRALS AND CHURCHES

PAUL E. HARDY

*With drawings by the author*

CONSTRUCTION PRESS
LONDON AND NEW YORK

Construction Press
an imprint of:
Longman Group Limited
Longman House, Burnt Mill, Harlow
Essex CM20 2JE, England
Associated companies throughout the world

*Published in the United States of America*
*by Longman Inc., New York*



*First published 1983*

**British Library Cataloguing in Publication Data**

Hardy, Paul E.
A guide to the care and preservation of medieval
cathedrals and churches.
1. Cathedrals 2. Church architecture
– Conservation and restoration
3. Architecture, Medieval – Conservation
and restoration
I. Title
726'6 NA4830

ISBN 0-582-30514-4

**Library of Congress Cataloging in Publication Data**

Hardy, Paul E., 1924–
A guide to the care and preservation of medieval cathedrals
and churches.
Includes index.
1. Cathedrals – Conservation and restoration.
2. Architecture, Medieval
– Conservation and restoration.
I. Title.
NA4830.H37 1983 726'.5'0880941 82-14257
ISBN 0-582-30514–4

Set in 10/11 pt Linotron 202 Bembo
Printed in Hong Kong by
Wilture Printing Co Ltd.

# Contents

# Preface

The desire to write this book has been with me for many years and for a number of reasons. I was born in a cathedral city and at an early age went to live in another city that is still regarded as one of the architectural gems of Europe. Growing up in this environment I soon became aware of the architectural heritage and realised what a permanent place it has in British history. For me it was the beginning of a life of investigation, appreciation and delight.

Half a century later the need to share these experiences urged me to express my enthusiasm and concern for the care and preservation of medieval ecclesiastical buildings, and hopefully awaken a similar response in others.

In writing this book it has never been my intention to present a complete textbook on the subject; there are many excellent books already available. What I hope to do is stimulate and encourage those who have a concern for these buildings, and at the same time provide certain basic facts and information enabling them to act in a responsible way.

I owe so much to so many people who have, by their creative ability, technical know-how, aesthetic awareness and commonsense, given me increasing pleasure and satisfaction when investigating medieval cathedrals and churches.

Conferences and seminars dealing with the care and preservation of historic buildings take place periodically and this is a necessary activity. Lectures and dialogues produce useful information and various societies are responsible for the distribution of this literature providing the data that instructs and guides those who are responsible for the fabric. They also issue warnings as to the right use of new materials and there are some who say that if there is doubt, don't do it! At all times we must be willing to consult the experts who are able to point in the right direction.

In putting this book together I must acknowledge the careful technical attention given by Colin Bassett, Carole Tuckett who typed and re-typed the text without a murmur and managed to have a baby between Chapters seven and eight, Martin Myhill, MA, ALA, who dealt with the index and got excited about it! My thanks are also due to the Bishop of Exeter who graciously accepted the job of writing the Foreword, and my wife who, sharing my enthusiasm, had to manage without me for long periods so that I could get on with the writing and drawing. For the errors and inadequacies which a work of this kind cannot entirely hope to escape, the responsibility is mine.

PEH
EXETER
DEVON

# Foreword by the Bishop of Exeter

We take for granted the continued existence of our cathedrals and parish churches – especially those of medieval origin. We value them for what they are – functional places in which God's honour dwells; places in which the local household of God meets regularly to worship God and to renew its life with his gifts; buildings of simple beauty or of compelling grandeur which evoke a sense of wonderment from those who have an eye to see beyond the functional; constructions that carry with them the almost subliminal factor of giving an identity to a local community of people; edifices in which craftsmanship has brought together stone, timber, glass and metal in such a manner as to create a symbol of the spiritual dimension which distinguishes human life from the sum of things.

In fact, it is almost incredible that we can still speak, in the most facile of clichés, of our 'rich inheritance'. The shrewdness of those who built – combined with the enlightened commonsense of generations of clergy, churchwardens and local craftsmen – these have stood fast against the inexorable effect of half a millennium of natural erosion.

Paul Hardy's book comes as a reminder to us that the taking for granted of what we have received will not, in future, suffice. Wood, lead, iron, mortar and stone are all vulnerable to decay and deterioration – most notably, perhaps, when they are in contrived conjunction with each other. His purpose is to highlight those points at which this vulnerability is most acute, and thereby to prompt those whose duty it is to care for these buildings to take timely action to conserve our heritage. I am happy to commend this book not only to those for whom it will hold technical interest but also to the many ordinary people at local level who will be best placed to detect the danger-spots and take the appropriate action.

# *Chapter 1*
# A glorious heritage

Long before arriving in a city or town in the Middle Ages the first things that came into view were spires and towers; such was the splendid architecture of church buildings. As well as being aesthetic, church architecture served a practical purpose, for the preaching of the word and the use of the liturgy was not the ultimate source of teaching. It was an age when the majority of the population could not read; nor could they understand Latin. It was, therefore, much more exciting to have instruction and experience expressed in tangible ways: by sculpture in stone, by artists who could make the Christian gospel understandable with colour and composition, and by the use of vaulted space that was a visual delight – all of which was supremely bonded in the total creation by the work of the master mason and his craftsmen. These itinerants, or 'travelling teams', as they were called, possessed a mixture of skills and abilities: some, known as 'hewers', worked the stone with axes and dressed it with chisels; some, called 'setters', would lay the walls and mix the mortar matrices; others, known as 'turners', would be responsible for shaping the column and the shaft with their stone-lathes. There were also glaziers, carvers, plumbers, smiths, slaters, joiners and wrights – craftsmen who took the raw materials, formed them into the required shapes, positioned them in appropriate places, lifted and shifted them until they were exact and filled the window spaces with patterned and coloured glass.

Before the Norman Conquest England was financially, socially and materially unsound, mainly because she was distant from the centre of European ideas. During the one hundred and fifty years that followed the invasion of William I, England became involved in the movements affecting the western world which included the struggle for communal liberty, the crusades, and the growth and development of towns. The Church was one of the first English institutions to profit from the

**Fig. 1.1** Late Norman church

changes that followed the Norman invasion. The French bishops who were given British appointments were familiar with the Romanesque churches on the continent and their first thought was to rebuild their cathedrals in the new style. In the villages and hamlets the Norman nobles built stone churches in place of the earlier buildings of thatch and wood. During the reigns of William the Conqueror, William Rufus and Henry I almost every cathedral was rebuilt from the foundations. The procedure involved rebuilding sections from the east end, and to achieve this the nave was often used as a church while the choir was being constructed. Around the apse a Lady chapel, or chapels, would be added. This work was often not of the highest standard due mainly to the limited ability of local labour, even though it was under the supervision of the Norman master masons.

A feature of the later, larger Norman churches was the cruciform shape, with a low tower at the intersection of the nave, choir and transepts (Fig. 1.1). The choir was usually short with only four bays: it had a semi-circular apse at the east end which was thought to be a sufficient area for Mass. The nave, usually unbroken, was extensive and roofed with painted wood; the walls were of rubble and mortar, substantially thick, and faced with cut stone. The columns (see Fig. 1.2) had a core of rubble and were faced with ashlar masonry, which gave the appearance of strength but had an innate weakness. The early Norman builders were aware of the limitations of their materials and tended to avoid any superstructure such as large windows or stone vaults.

The developments of planning and building also saw corresponding changes in sculpture and decoration. The single slab of stone which served as a lintel for a door opening (Fig. 1.3) in the smaller churches

Fig. 1.2 Norman nave column with chevron decoration

**Fig. 1.3** Stone lintel

of the Saxon period became quite inadequate when processional rituals took place, and thus the arch developed. The doorways received special treatment, and were widened and decorated. Clustered piers were devised to replace double columns as the pier was advantageous in so far as the arch harmonised with its support. The piers and arches of this period were decorated with carved mouldings, the most notable being the zig-zag or chevron (Figs 1.2 and 1.4). There were also the billet, the star, the lozenge (Fig. 3.10), the abacus and the string; in fact, at the end of the Norman period decoration became very profuse.

These churches were built at the same time as the cathedrals and took pride of place in the community. As they were skilfully and carefully built, it is not surprising that they are in such good condition today, and are still standing. Piers and columns were both used (Fig. 1.5), the columns being circular on plan and the piers square. The piers were occasionally shafted with heavy half-columns. The capitals were substantially larger than the column or pier in order to provide a greater area from which the arch could spring; it also gave the opportunity to ornament the junction. The examples that remain are large and austere. The top piece, the abacus, is a square or round block of stone, to which mouldings were added at a later date. The bases of Early Norman columns were usually substantial plinths (Fig. 1.6); they also had mouldings at a later date.

Norman windows were small compared to the large doors; and the early versions were in fact not much more than slits between 3 in.

**Fig. 1.4** Chevron decoration

**Fig. 1.5** Norman nave pier

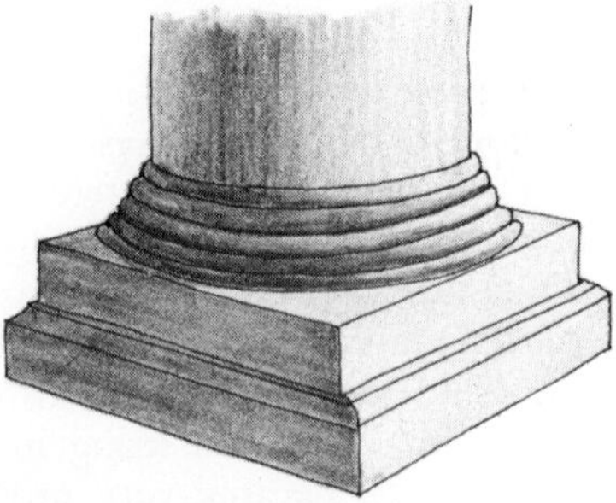

**Fig. 1.6** Plinth and column

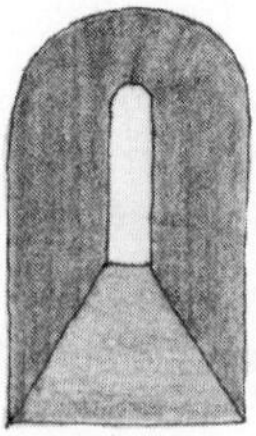

**Fig. 1.7** Norman window

(76 mm) and 4 in. (102 mm) wide with rounded heads. (Fig. 1.7). The narrow windows were mainly for defence purposes; they were set near the outer wall surface and were deeply splayed from the interior. They were eventually widened with round heads and carved mouldings in concentric semi-circles, and had shafts at the sides. Some of these windows were divided into two lights by a central shaft.

The roof coverings during this period were of stone or tiled slates, wood shingles or thatch, and were fixed to a steeply pitched roof that would reject water and snow quickly (Fig. 1.8.) The later introduction of lead covering allowed the roof to be much flatter. The roof overhung the walls and was supported at the top of the wall by a cornice which rested on corbels (Fig. 1.9.) This unit is known as a corbel table. Above the corbel table was a parapet of two thicknesses

**Fig. 1.8** Steeply pitched roofs

**Fig. 1.9** Stone-carved corbel

**Fig. 1.10** Gargoyle

of stone with a lead lining between. Openings were made at certain intervals to allow the rainwater to escape. To prevent the rainwater from discharging down the face of the wall, lead spouts were fixed and inserted into stone blocks, which in turn became features as gargoyles in the most interesting, and sometimes hideous, shapes such as animals, fish, monsters and devils (see Fig. 1.10.)

Most Norman roofs were constructed of timber. In the smaller churches the structure was uncovered, showing rafters and ridge piece. Purlins and wall plates were supported by stone corbels at the top of the wall. The rafters ran across at right angles to the main beams and a substantial tie-beam ran from wall to wall at intervals to counteract the outward thrust of the roof (Fig. 1.11).

The Romans had covered their wide spans with stone and concrete, and this type of interior span was known as a vault. Barrel vaults (Fig. 1.12), however, were constructed by the Saxons and Early Nor-

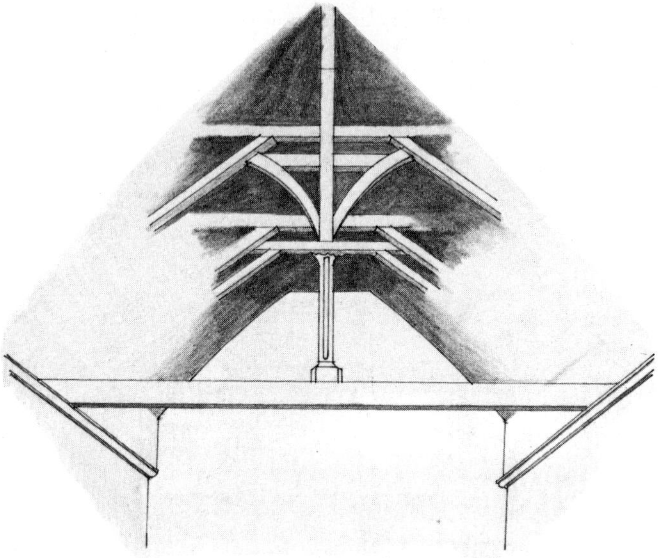

**Fig. 1.11** Tie-beam and king post

**Fig. 1.12** Barrel vault

man builders to cover smaller spans, such as aisles. The barrel vault was followed by the groined and ribbed vault (Fig. 1.13), the latter being associated more with the Gothic period but used by the Normans. The thrust in groined and ribbed vaulting is concentrated along the diagonal ribs, thus giving force at the points on the wall just above the arch springing where the counter-thrust is needed. A simple flying-buttress system (Fig. 1.14) was used, which could not be seen on the exterior – as was the case in later Gothic architecture – but was visible in the triforia passages.

Low, wide Norman towers are quite distinctive (Fig. 1.15). At the top is an embattled parapet with gargoyle spouts and at each corner is a turret. These towers are ornamented on all four faces with arcading, slit window and, at a later date, belfry openings. The low, wooden spires that surmounted the tower have, in most instances, disappeared (Fig. 1.16).

The transition from the Norman to the Early English style of architecture is approximately equivalent to the transition from

**Fig. 1.13** Groined and ribbed vault

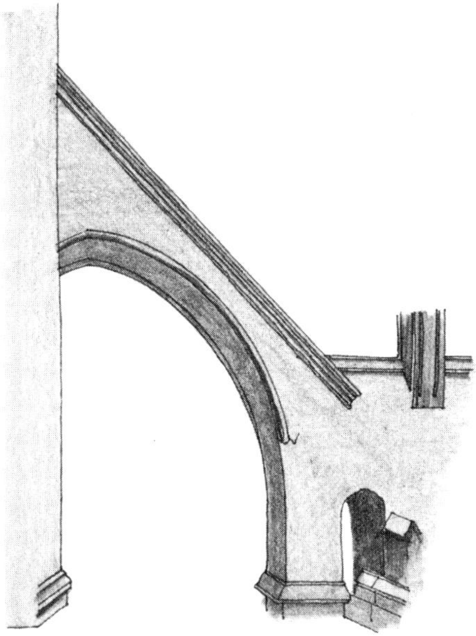

**Fig. 1.14** Flying buttress

Romanesque to Gothic in France and Germany. The difference between Norman and Gothic is not defined by the absence or presence of any architectural feature; it is more a difference of mood than of craft. The Norman Church was significant, and in some ways exerted a

**Fig. 1.15** Late Norman tower

**Fig. 1.16** Low, wooden spire

great deal of power, but it was not destined to enshrine the enthusiasm of medieval England.

Ecclesiastical architecture, which became known as Gothic, emerged from Romanesque/Norman style. It was gradual, and although architectural historians have divided it into certain phases, these dates seem to vary and overlap. We see stone-ribbed vaults (Fig. 1.17), pointed arches (Fig. 1.18) and flying buttresses (Fig. 1.14) and there is a tendency to label them. They were not entirely new, however; and in many cases they were a fusion of several factors from the past. What it did achieve represented a new artistic and structural expression. It was influenced by Christianity and was an essential ingredient in the life of the people, with the result that the community put all their effort into building structures to the Glory of God. These

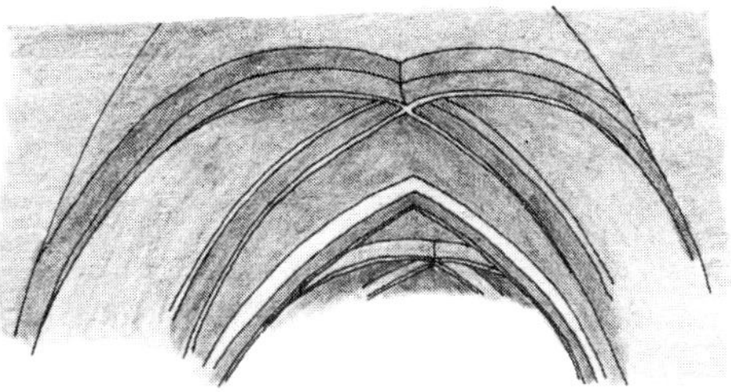

**Fig. 1.17** Stone-ribbed vaults

**Fig. 1.18** Pointed arches

**Fig. 1.19** Decorated Gothic

structures – from obscure parish churches to cathedrals – became very important buildings and, in consequence, there were contributions of time and skill as well as money. In return, the churches offered education, refuge and interest, which made sense of what the people were being taught to believe. Many great things happen in life because there is need, and fortunately the ability is usually available to create and develop materials to turn that requirement into reality as people fulfil their desires and aspirations.

As the Gothic period developed, ecclesiastical buildings became larger in capacity and closer to heaven in structure (Fig. 1.19). The doorways and windows (Fig. 1.20 and 1.21) were increased in size, which meant that interiors were illuminated by natural light, giving the buildings a new visual dimension. As structural knowledge increased, the techniques improved, especially in the development of the vault

**Fig. 1.20** Doorway

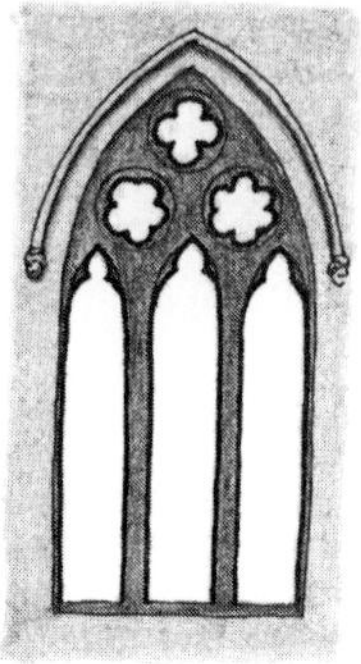

**Fig. 1.21** Window

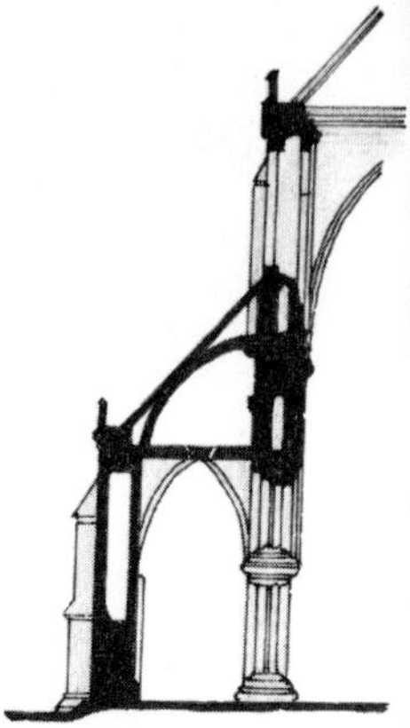

**Fig. 1.22** Buttress and vault

and all its associated items. The buttress shown in Fig. 1.22 is complementary to the vault; the higher the vault, the greater the buttress. In this way the mason provided the correct reinforcement at the right place, just beneath the springing line of the vault. The success of the buttress owes as much to its visual result as it does to its structural soundness.

These buildings, be they large or small, are remarkable in their workmanship. When we enter, we marvel that they were built eight hundred years ago. Men had to climb very high scaffolding to position each stone as weeks became months and months became years. The chosen site had to be sufficiently level to build on as no instrumentation was available. Levels were usually determined by taking a sighting on some focal point in the distance. This system was improved when water was used in a container – a forerunner of the spirit-level. As in architecture of every age, it was essential to commence properly, and the medieval builders were no exception; they set their buildings on a plinth, not just for appearance but essentially as a base and on this kind of platform the monument of stone was dependent.

Bases, piers and capitals are integral parts of the interior of ecclesiastical buildings and the mouldings and ornaments become a useful guide in identifying phases in Gothic architecture (Fig. 1.23). These designs changed rapidly in style which often meant that the characteristics also changed. Between 1150 and 1550 there was a tendency to have tall bases, slender piers and capitals that were grouped.

A contrast in colour was achieved by the use of different materials, especially in the Early English piers. One of the materials frequently used in cathedrals was dark Purbeck marble. The capitals, which were foliated and surmounted by a round abacus, were somewhat severe (Fig. 1.24).

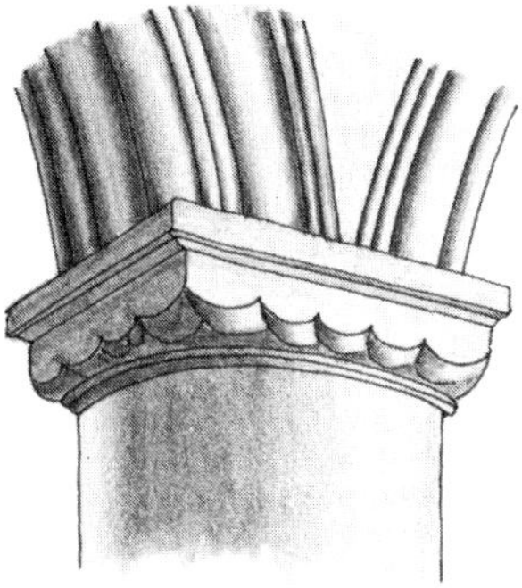

**Fig. 1.23** Capital

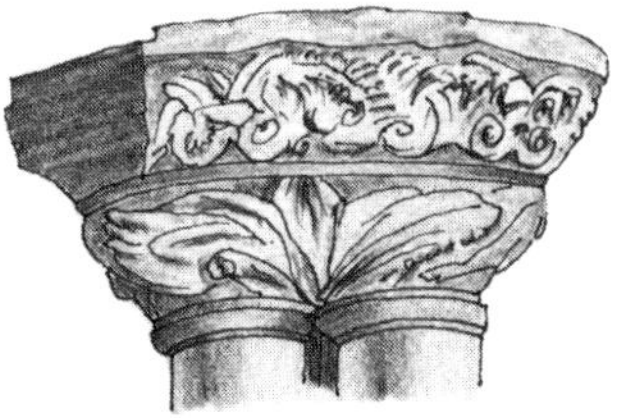

**Fig. 1.24** Foliated capital

Piers of the fourteenth century were designed with a central shaft surrounded by more slender shafts. The capitals were carved sensitively and appeared natural with a profusion of fruit and flowers. In the Perpendicular phase the piers were much thinner, and the vaulting shafts which carry up the front and back of the piers in an unbroken line from floor to vault were particularly attractive. The capitals were often plain in small buildings but carved in the larger structures (Fig. 1.25). There was, however, more style: they were lower in relief and included foliage and figures. The bases were high and thin, and quite often bell-shaped with an octagonal plinth.

The mouldings and ornaments of the Early English phase referred to above were deep cut, resulting in strong shadows. The ornament itself was restrained and the mouldings were delicately carved. The most typical ornamental motif of the Early English phase is the dog-tooth, which can be described as a small pyramid in shape, cut into four leaves and repeated (Fig. 1.26).

Some other typical designs are the diaper and the crocket. In the Decorated phase the ball flower became a very popular motif: it was an attractive globular shape with the flower partly open (Fig. 1.27). Frequent use was made of the roll and ogee mouldings in the Perpendicular phase. The distinctive design could be seen in the panel form on all surfaces and the crockets were delicately carved with the mouldings shallow and broad (Fig. 1.28).

The three essential factors in medieval building – abutments, vaults and roofs – are interdependent to the whole design. An abutment (Fig. 1.29) was vital to obtain the stability required in a stone-vaulted roof. If timber was used in the construction of the roof, the abutment was of less importance.

Because of the development of Gothic architecture it was necessary to use stone in the vaulting, partly to reduce the risk of fire, but also to give flexibility. The vaults became ribbed, and as they were higher and wider they required extended abutment. Abutment was the exter-

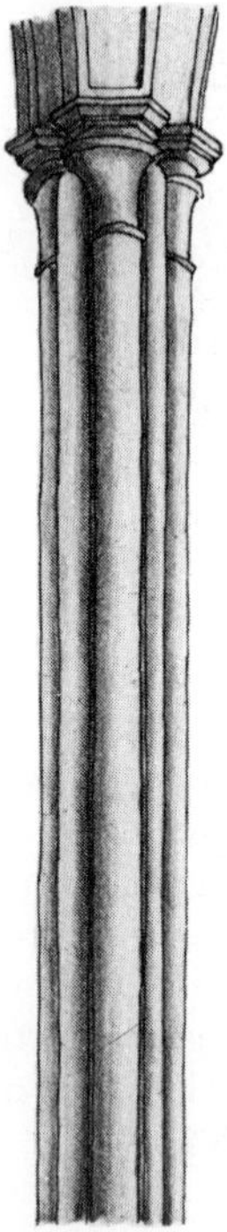

**Fig. 1.25** Perpendicular pier

**Fig. 1.26** Ornamental motif: dog tooth

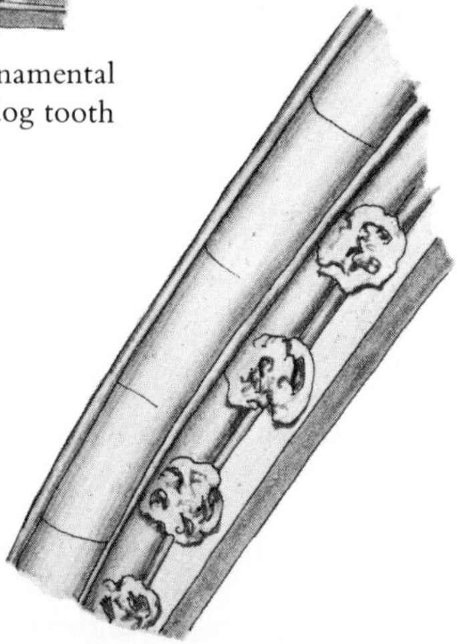

**Fig. 1.27** Ball flower

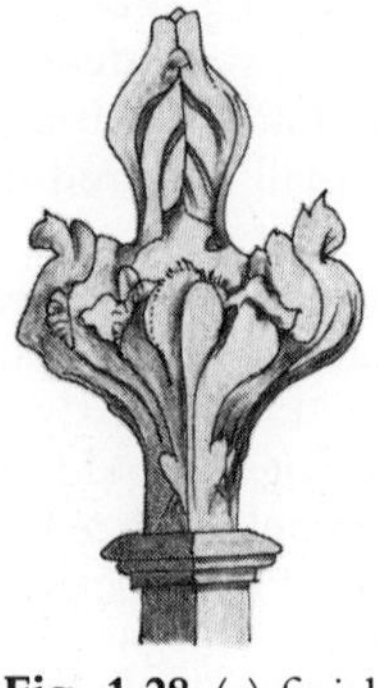

**Fig. 1.28** (a) finial (b) crocket

nal strengthening of the wall at the point where the greatest thrust took place. From this source the flying buttress was developed to provide strength at this particular point. The flying buttress also gave a counter-thrust on the external wall face which carried the vault pressure away from the building and down to the ground. A heavy pinnacle was placed on top to offset the thrust of the vault (Fig. 1.30).

The designs of the earliest Gothic vaults were formed by ribs with a quadripartite pattern; i.e. four ribs crossing diagonally forming four

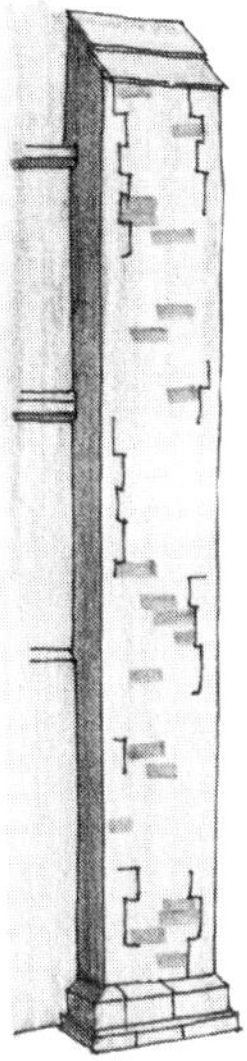

**Fig. 1.29** Abutment

**Fig. 1.30** Flying-buttress detail

**Fig. 1.31** Quadripartite

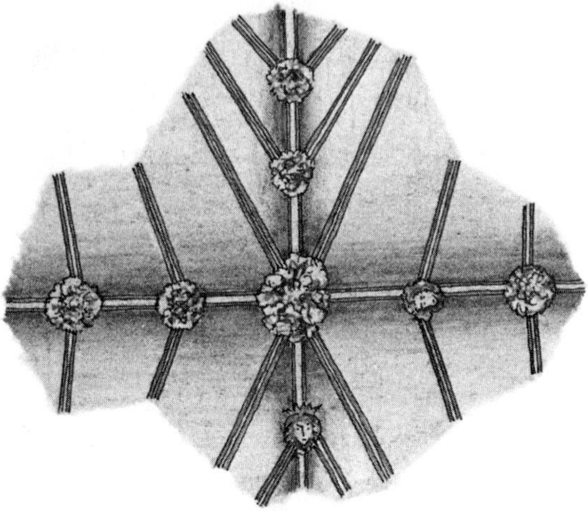

**Fig. 1.32** Tierceron

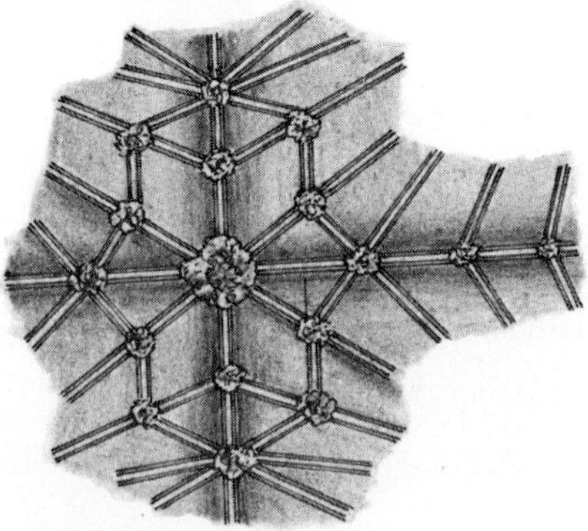

**Fig. 1.33** Lierne

compartments (Fig. 1.31). With this as a basic pattern the design became more intricate. Intermediate ribs known as tiercerons (see Fig. 1.32) were introduced, which extended from the vault springing to the rib at the ridge. This development occurred in the fourteenth century and the style is typical of this phase of architecture. Shortly afterwards the lierne vault shown in Fig. 1.33 evolved. In this very involved geometry, the structural ribs extended in any direction to join other ribs.

The Perpendicular phase had an English design. The fan vault (Fig. 1.34) had ribs of different curves springing from the capital, elaborately designed as a series of stone fans. The ribs which radiated from the fan were of equal length and the bounding line formed a semi-circle. Such a grouping of ribs created an inverted concave cone. A feature of this architectural phase was the minimum amount of wall

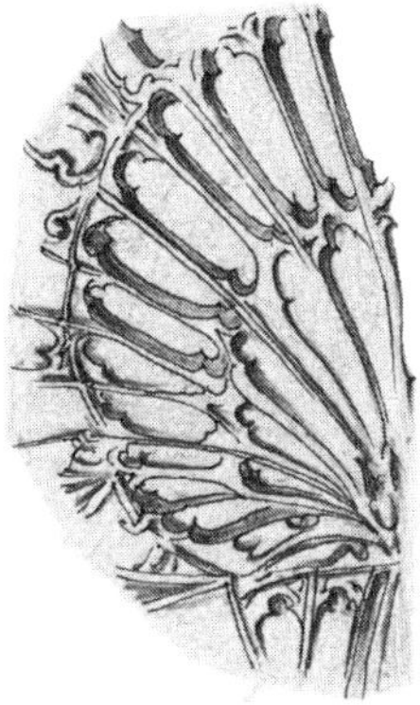

**Fig. 1.34** Fan vault

**Fig. 1.35** Window area complemented by vault

space and the large amount of window area complemented by vaults of large proportions (Fig. 1.35).

The building activities of the Normans were brisk. Later in the Middle Ages much of their work was altered and the early medieval churches were built on either cruciform or rectangular plan (Fig. 1.36). Single or twin western towers replaced the Normans' 'cross' design, the eastern apse was superseded by a square end, and the chancel was extended to give more space for the chapels that would be used for private prayers. The addition of aisles to some of the naves required the raising of nave walls into which clerestory windows were inserted. Of the many parish churches that were enlarged in the fourteenth century (Fig. 1.37), most of them retained their timber roofs and were covered by a variety of materials such as lead, tiles, wood, shingles, thatch, etc.

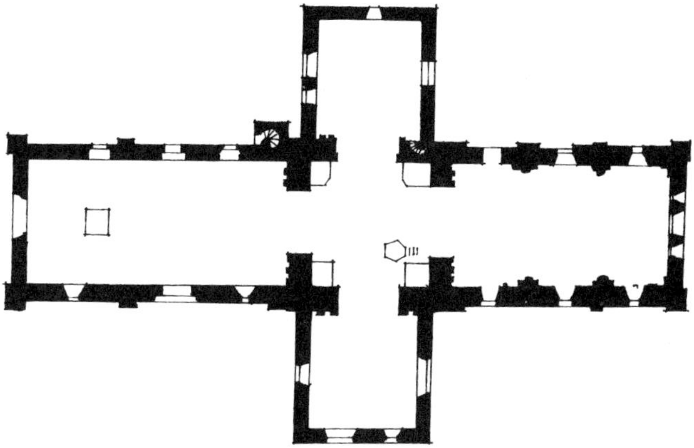

**Fig. 1.36** Cruciform plan

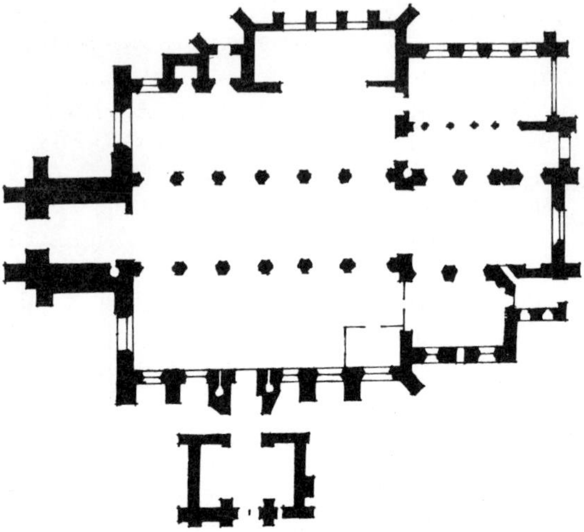

**Fig. 1.37** Church enlarged

**Fig. 1.38** Tower

**Fig. 1.39** Spire

From 1375 to 1550, which was one of the most notable periods of this particular British heritage, the variety of materials used was very often determined by the region. Stone was the most prominent material, with granite and flint being used extensively where available. Towers (Fig. 1.38) and spires (Fig. 1.39) were features in the Early English phase and throughout the medieval period; they were mainly decorative and gave aesthetic delight. They were often the result of desires of grandeur by those who wished the elegance of their buildings to be noticed.

The cathedrals and churches in Britain were built for the worship of God and their worth far exceeds any human definition. They are some of the greatest buildings of our architectural heritage, and within their walls are many of our most historical and artistic treasures. We are fortunate that for centuries the land has been free of invasion and civil strife, and we are also fortunate to have had numerous generations who were dedicated to the care and preservation of such a varied and rich collection of ecclesiastical buildings. The profusion of architectural beauty scattered throughout the land creates and maintains the stimulant to keep values and hopes alive. These cathedrals and churches may have a basic similarity, but each has an intrinsic beauty of its own.

# *Chapter 2*
# Architectural and constructional details

The previous chapter has taken a broad sweep through the architectural periods that are our main concern in the care and preservation of ecclesiastical buildings. In this chapter it is necessary to examine and consider more closely some of the details of the architectural features and their construction. There are several major structural items – such as support, roofing, abutment and natural lighting – that influenced the builders in the various methods that were taken (a) to shape the vaults, (b) to keep them properly supported, (c) to ensure that the outward thrust was counteracted and (d) to ensure that natural lighting was satisfactory. Simultaneously, each of these features was always involved in interplay; for example, the need for better natural lighting required larger windows and, consequently, the increase in height determined the support of the aisle and clerestory walls. The rapid way in which the skill of the masons evolved made it possible not only to build higher structures and realise greater space but also to do so by a real economy of material – something the masons always wanted to achieve. An important factor in every building of this period was that all the main features could be structurally justified – with a few exceptions, such as tall towers, which could cause problems. When considering the constructional planning of a building, the first aspect was the span of the roof, and this applied whether stone arches, or vaulting, or coupled rafters or timber beams were used. Since building science was being given serious attention, it was determined that some formulae, such as a building unit, should be considered in setting out the structures. When the medieval craftsmen had worked out a solution – sometimes several solutions – no time was wasted in their application.

One of these 'solutions' was the principle of dividing the building into bays and stories (Fig. 2.1), which would be given emphasis by

Fig. 2.1 Bays and storeys

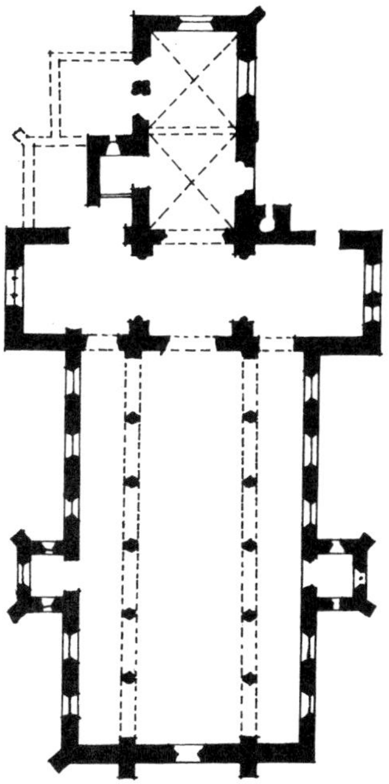

**Fig. 2.2** The introduction of aisles

architectural features. The early timber building bay unit was indicated by the spacing of principal posts. In the twelfth century, the overall projection of an aisle in relation to the main structure frequently equals the bay unit or what is now called the module. The span, although originally intended to be twice the module, could vary a great deal; the standard of measurement could vary from region to region. Basically two measurements were used: the 'pole' and the 'stick'. The pole was used for the plan of the structure, was considered to be 16 ft (4.8 m) long, and was determined originally by asking sixteen men to stand with their right foot, toe to heel, one behind the other. For the purpose of building they used the 'stick', which was 4 ft (1.2 m) long.

We can be fairly certain that the Anglo-Saxon foot was almost the same as the Imperial foot with which we are familiar; the pole of 16 ft and 'stick' subdivisions of 4 ft appear in many of the plans of that period. Measurements taken of buildings erected after the Conquest indicate that the foot was then equal to one and one-eighth of the Imperial foot, and by the end of the twelfth century the modern foot seems to have been in use. When the masons took over, a new

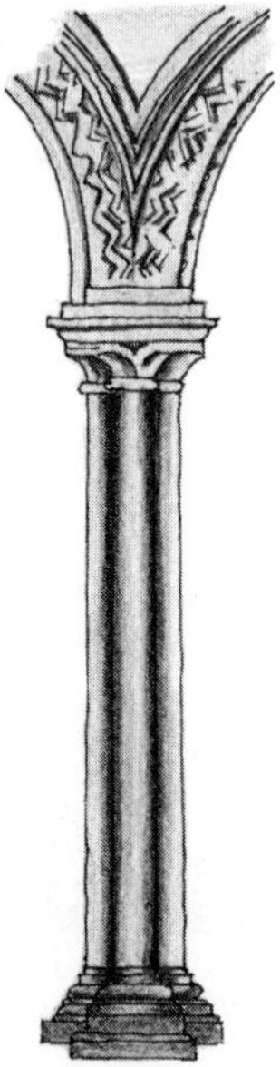

**Fig. 2.3** Stone piers

**Fig. 2.4** Arcuated: arches across spans

measurement was introduced, which was identified by the marks on the iron squares of the hewers. This was the basic inch, but as this could also vary, the main courses required a template.

The planning by bays was extended when aisles were introduced (see Fig. 2.2), due mainly to the plans of buildings which were supported by timber posts – a Byzantine feature. This was acknowledged by the early builders who concluded that it was possible to build a wall that could be supported on arches. This required stone piers which would be linked at the top by arches (Fig. 2.3).

Medieval architecture had a particular style known as 'arcuated', which meant that the openings had arches across the spans (as shown in Fig. 2.4) and not lintels as seen in the classical and ancient style. To allow an arch to be turned, it is necessary to have a strong and firmly supported centring of timber. The wall above, if it is thick, will also require a corresponding thickness in centring. In the eleventh century the English builders found that they could turn their arches in widening rings known as 'orders', each of which became a centre of a wider ring above. This was repeated until the full thickness of the wall was achieved, and as this development proved to be very successful it contributed greatly to the effectiveness of

**Fig. 2.5** Piers with flat soffits

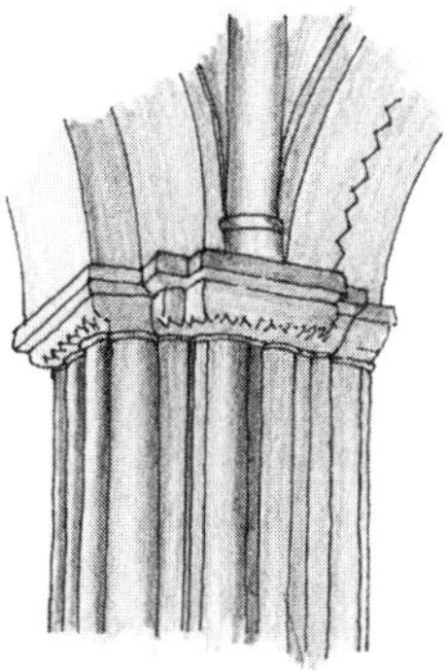

**Fig. 2.6** Compound pier

Early English Gothic. The pointed arch, which had been in existence since the Anglo-Saxon era, was easily accepted into English architecture as it was shaped by the masons (Fig. 1.18).

At first masonry arcades were achieved by cutting holes in the wall of a building in order to obtain extra accommodation. Later buildings were erected with aisles, the main walls being incorporated and supported on an arcade that had very substantial stone piers which usually had flat soffits, the same thickness as the wall (Fig. 2.5). This developed into the 'ordered' arch and was supported by a 'compound' pier. The half-column disappeared and was replaced by groups of two or three half-shafts which were slender and graceful (Fig. 2.6).

When ribbed vaulting was introduced (see Fig. 1.17), additional shafts that were to carry the ribs were added to the pier design. By the middle of the eleventh century the Anglican masons built duplex-bay arcades; that is, alternating piers and columns (Fig. 2.7).

It was not until the twelfth century that the masons of England began to build columns with stone drums, each with four shafts of marble from Purbeck, and such shafts may well be a development from the design of wooden posts which were used in the timber churches.

**Fig. 2.7** Duplex bay

The function of these walls is to support the roof. The construction of the roof is composed of rafters inclined towards each other at the apex and resting on the wall plate (Fig. 2.8). This could create problems as it was necessary to prevent the substantial weight of the roof-covering from forcing the apex of the roof downwards, causing the rafters that were bearing on the wall to move outwards. In order to combat this, various forms of bracing were used on each pair of rafters. In most of the early medieval roofs the final solution was to use a single horizontal tie-beam known as a 'collar' (Fig. 1.11). The braces and collars used later were improved by two wall plates, one to support the foot of the rafters and the other to support a short vertical timber. This was in fact, a brace between the foot of the rafter and the top of the thick medieval wall.

Trusses (Fig. 2.9), developed to support the ridges, were based mainly on the form of the timber cruck (Fig. 2.10). In its original form this was primitive, but it developed and by the late medieval period elaborate timber frames were used. The truss was not limited

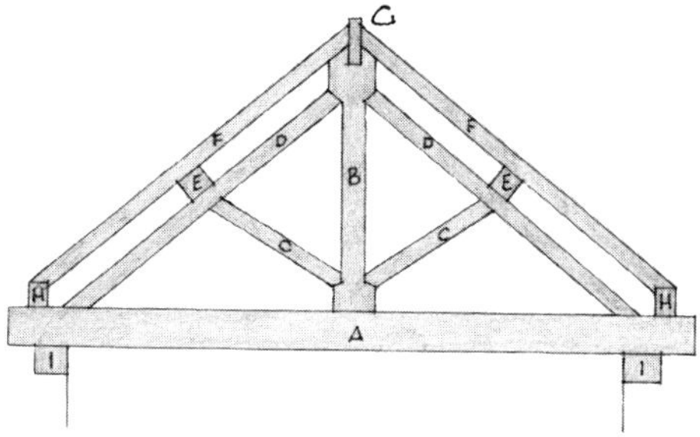


**Fig. 2.8** Construction of roof

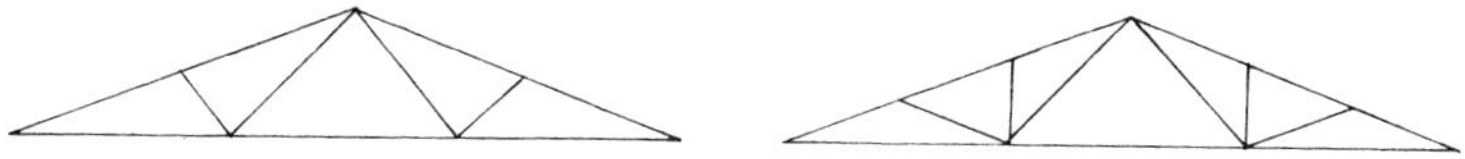

**Fig. 2.9** Trusses

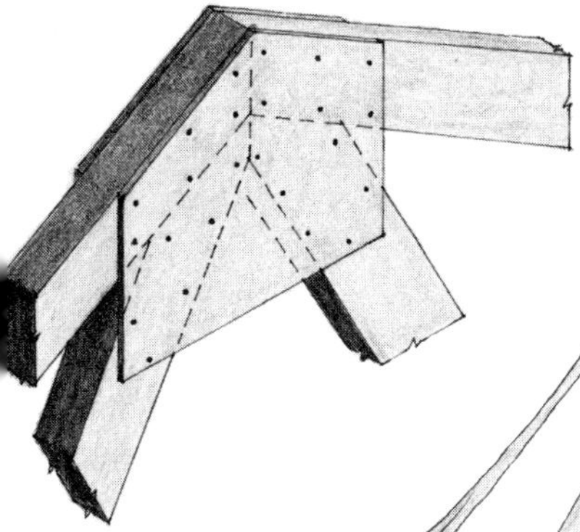

**Fig. 2.10** Timber cruck

to supporting the ridge piece, it also had to bear the purlins (Fig. 2.11) which ran parallel to the wall plate. The purlins reinforced the rafters to prevent them from sagging under the weight of

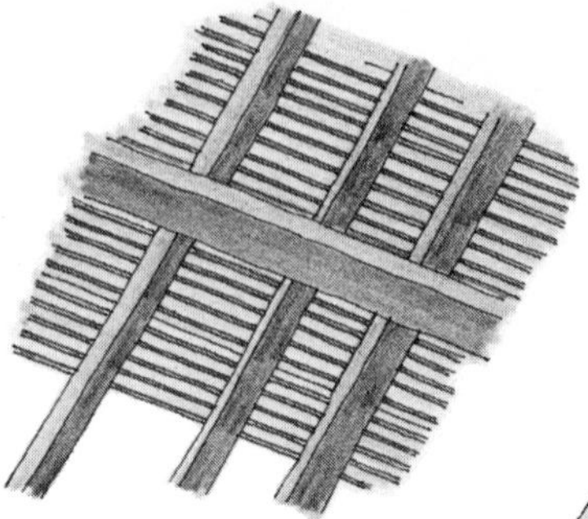

**Fig. 2.11** Purlins

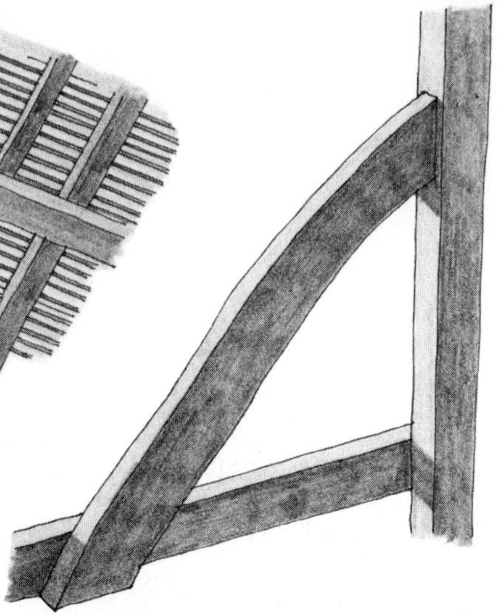

**Fig. 2.12** Arch brace

slates which could become very heavy over an area. With this kind of pressure provision had to be made to prevent the roof from collapsing, and small arched braces were used (Fig. 2.12) to join the trusses and purlins. As roof construction developed the tie-beam (Fig. 1.11) took over the main role. The king post (Fig. 2.13) was intrinsic in the design and it produced a principle not unlike the roof truss of classical days. Eventually the tie-beam functioned as the principal beam due to the pitch of the roof being almost flat.

The timber framework of medieval roofs is but the basis for the actual roof covering. The whole character of Gothic architecture changed when the roof pitches were lowered. The soaring arches had reached their peak about the middle of the thirteenth century, but they too were reduced. The bay unit was widened as the church designers of England were not as ambitious as their French counterparts; in England the aim was to design for economy of structure, e.g. in the use of slender columns. Widening the span meant that the springing line had to be modified, thus reducing the pitch of the arch; alternatively, it required the entire feature to be made much higher. In the greater churches the ceilings were boarded (Fig. 2.14) for reasons best known to the builders, who said that they could not have their most important spans vaulted and that it covered up the mixture of roof timbers. There was a prevailing school of thought which was certain that it prevented fire in the roof, but the obvious question is 'What could be more inflammable than a timber roof concealed by a ceiling built of wood?'

Vaulting, like arcading, was a legacy from the buildings of the Ro-

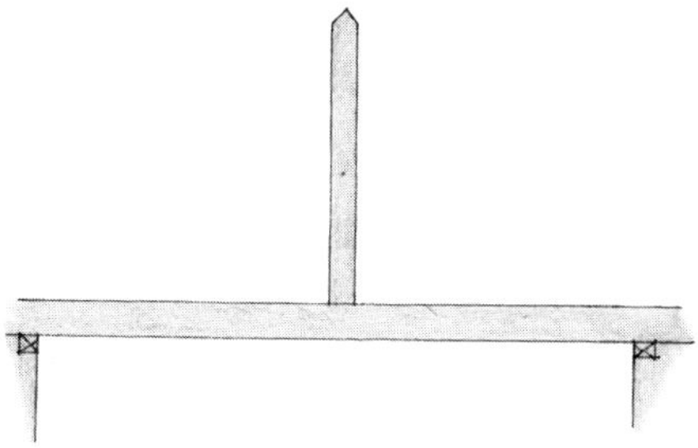

**Fig. 2.13** King post

**Fig. 2.14** Boarded ceiling

nans – their schemes being carried out in concrete. It was common-place to use this method of construction on small spans, such as beneath the galleries over the aisles of the larger churches. The stone vault was expensive and laborious and was at first confined to those who could afford it. Its development indicates the medieval striving fter lightness and economy of material, but with the additional aim of minimising, as far as possible, the use of temporary wooden centring during construction, which was expensive and troublesome to prepare and supply. Many of the steps taken had been initially devised to give the masons less trouble, but when they had worked heir way to a mastery of the art in all its intricate flexibility, they were justifiably proud of their skill and enthusiastically went to the tmost limits of complexity, apparently ignoring the enormous ıbour involved.

The oldest and simplest form of vault is the 'barrel' type Fig. 1.12), which is not a familiar sight in England except in classical buildings. A barrel vault needs continuous abutment and, therefore, must be continuously supported by thick walls. One of the problems connected with barrel-vaulted structures is that it is difficult to provide window space. If windows were required they had o be set down beneath the springing of the vault to avoid the

**Fig. 2.15** Arched rib

necessity of cutting into this part. If two barrel vaults intersect, a groined vault is created. If this intersecting is repeated along a serie of rectangular compartments, a system of vaulting is created whicl gives an advance on the barrel in that the thrust is concentrated oı the four points of the springing.

These, however, are still very heavy, the groins are not particu larly strong, and each compartment must be constructed to set as solid mass. This involved a good deal of timber centring which wa expensive and difficult to make with the primitive wood-shapin tools of the Anglo-Saxon craftsmen. Profiting by the experienc obtained in the construction of arches with 'orders', the builders o the late eleventh century built the lines of the groining in narrov stone arches, forming ribs upon which vaulting would be con structed later.

The greatest step in the development of the vault was the intro duction of the arched rib (Fig. 2.15). The masons had always hope to be able to build stone ceilings that would cover large spans. Thi provided fresh problems: the mechanics were complicated, and th timber centring would be vast and high above the floor. Un daunted, the masons persevered and the introduction of the vaultin rib meant that they had overcome their problem in the first half o the twelfth century.

Let us look at the vault more closely and appreciate its parts. Th parts between the ribs are known as the web (Fig. 2.16). Frencl and English masons had different methods of filling the web witl masonry. The former would take the blocks of stone (Fig. 2.17 and work them to the special shapes needed to give a straight joint a

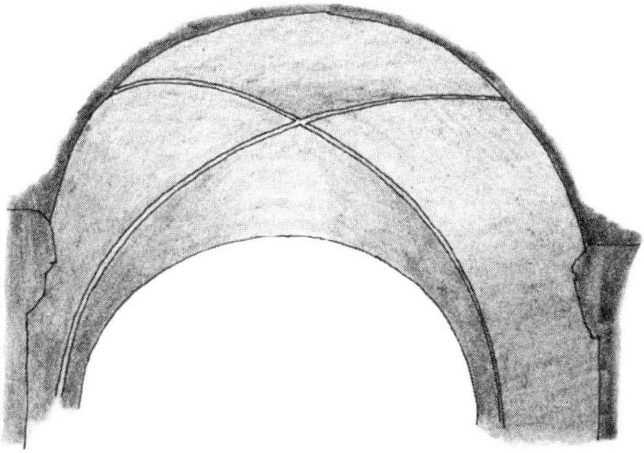

**Fig. 2.16** Rib web

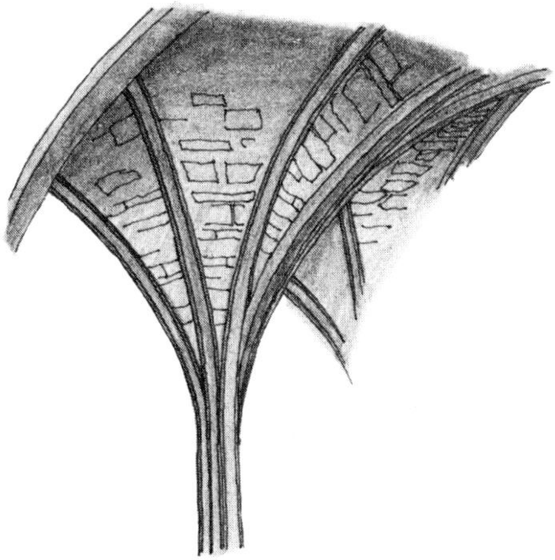

**Fig. 2.17** Rib web

the top of the cell, which continued to form a perfect arch across each vaulting compartment. The latter used blocks of stone of a standard size (Fig. 2.18) producing a ragged joint on the top. They swept their stones together, which meant that they laid them at right angles to the lines bisecting the sides of the vaulting bay and ridge ribs (Fig. 2.18). In this method the jointing of the vaulting webs which converged from each side of the vaulting compartment came together at the summit to form a serrated line. This was considered by some to be clever masonry; others thought it unsightly with the result that a ridge rib (Fig. 2.19) was used to cover the junction. Another ridge was introduced transversely in the centre of the bay of each vault – a type of vaulting known as 'quadripartite' (Fig. 1.31). In this method each bay is vaulted in four compartments which are separated by diagonal ribs. With this as a basis, another transverse rib

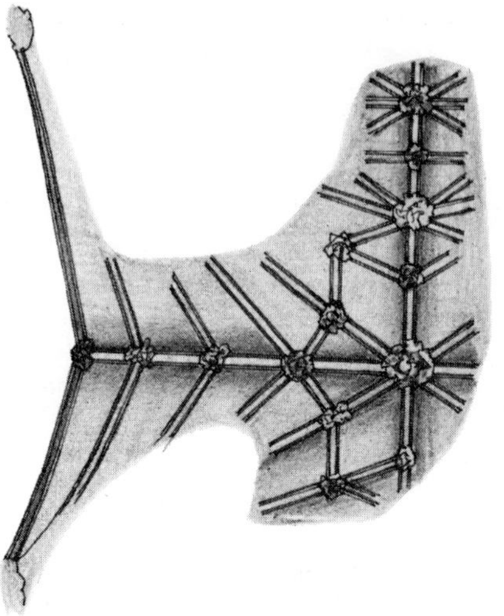

**Fig. 2.18** Bisecting sides of bay and vaulting

was introduced which created the bay design through two smaller arches on the side walls in place of a single large arch.

Where a multiplicity of ribs converged on a vault shaft, the lower courses were cut from one stone; this, in fact, became a corbel (Fig. 1.9) which, when bonded into the wall, was immensely strong. As it was difficult to mitre ribs at their intersection, a 'boss' of appropriate size was set; this was carved with figures and foliage, providing a continuous commentary on a story in the Bible or a religious theme (Fig. 2.20). The later builders proved themselves to be quite capable of mitring the most complicated vaults.

It seems that the development of the English vault was a constant experiment and the builders were not content to rely on their quadri-

**Fig. 2.19** Ridge rib

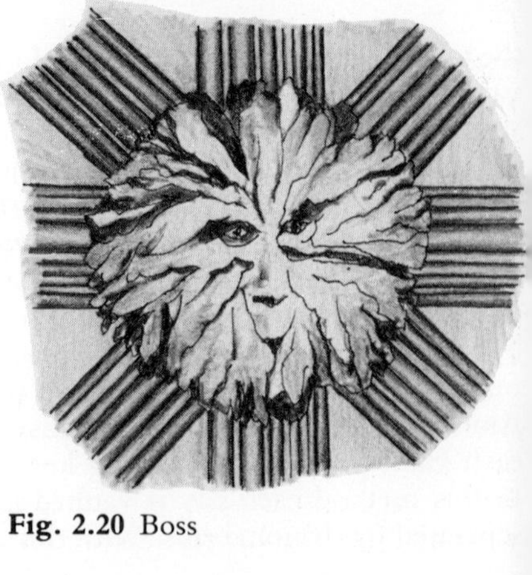

**Fig. 2.20** Boss

partite or sexpartite designs. They soon began to try additional ribs, called 'tiercerons' (Fig. 1.32). First came longitudinal ridge ribs then, sometimes, transverse ones. The four cells in pairs could also be provided with additional intersecting ribs which started at the shaft corners and joined either or both of the ridge ribs. These came into general use during the thirteenth century and were invariable in English practice. This effectively subdivided the areas to be filled and facilitated construction, while strengthening the vault and adding to the attractiveness of its appearance. The next stage was the 'lierne' vault, (Fig. 1.33) in which an additional number of ribs are connected to the main ribs but are not joined to the four nodal points of the shafts. The name arises from the French *lier*, to tie. They served no constructional purpose except to reduce the size of the subsection to be filled, but they opened the way to greater elaboration of decorative patterns.

The final phase of vaulting in England was reached when the number of ribs, which passed in all directions, had increased so much that there was no alternative but to combine the rib and the web into one stone. This meant that there was a substantial mass of masonry which was cleverly constructed to produce almost any shape desired. At the end of the fifteenth century it became known as 'fan' vaulting, and was an exclusive English feature (Fig. 1.34).

One important characteristic of the fan vault is that through any one point there are curvatures in opposite senses; that is, convex in one way and concave in the other. It is very rigid and the assumed deflection is small. As stone has low tensile strength, and as it is virtually impossible for stones to slip between each other, the stone structure will be stable as long as a line of thrust can be found within the masonry. The fan vault must have continuous support at its bottom and along its edges if it is to maintain equilibrium. The effective section of the fan vault is that part of the conoid represented in the lower courses of stone, the beds of which are horizontal, or from above the rubble-fill in the vaulting pockets to the central spandrel panel. The construction of these vaults was basic: in the first place the lower courses of stone were laid in each corner of the bay. These usually rested on the shafts which were securely set into the walls and in some ways functioned as corbels. This was followed by the wall ribs with their keystones. It was usual for the wall ribs to be inserted into indentations in the walls to provide a fixing, but this had problems because it was possible for a fracture to appear between the first course of vaulting stones and the wall ribs. The stones had to find their own level with one another and with the abutments. When the wall ribs were completed, the cone shape was developed and defined by the ribs progressing upwards in horizontal courses, and the transverse ridge stones were positioned at the same time. Finally, the central spandrel panel was put into place, which required a good deal of centring and was not without its problems. One of

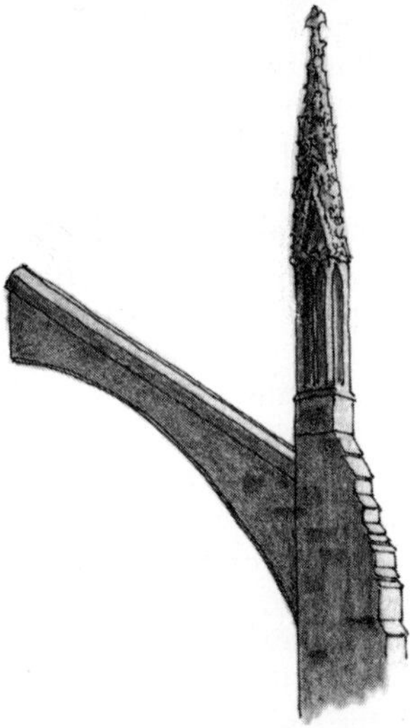

**Fig. 2.21** Buttress, pinnacle and flyer

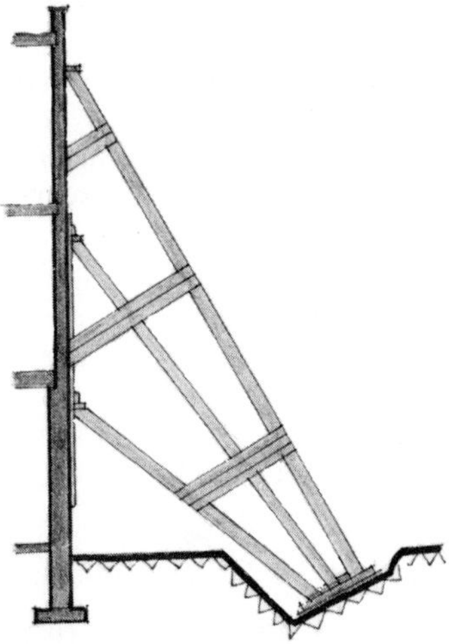

**Fig. 2.22** Typical raking shore

the final operations in construction was the carving of the ribs, which were probably started in the workshop, taken to a certain stage, placed in position and then completed. This process was necessary: if they had been completed in the workshop before being positioned, the compression would cause distortion and the stones would be out of line. The fan vault is a supreme achievement; it is technically brilliant and lovely to look at.

One of the main effects aimed for in churches was height. As the walls became higher they had to be increased in thickness not only to support the weight above but also the thrusts of the vaulting and roofs. When the groined vault (Fig. 1.13) was introduced, the thrust was concentrated on definite points on the walls corresponding to the bay divisions.

The erection of a building is only part of the operation; it has to be built in such a way that it stays up! At first, in church architecture, walls, piers, arches, etc. were massive, but when the era of this Romanesque characteristic was over, the concentration was on height and light. The larger window openings required support to ensure that they stood erect, and it was necessary to work out a nicely balanced adjustment of the buttress, pinnacle and flyer to counteract the spring-like kick or thrust of central and side vaults (Fig. 2.21). On the whole it was achieved, if empirically, with real success and very few structural failures are recorded. We see today that a building that is without support from its adjacent structures is prevented from toppling by raking shoring (Fig. 2.22), which transfers the floor and wall loads to the ground by means of sloping struts or rakers. The Gothic buttress is a stone version of this arrangement (see Fig. 1.22). As a vault is a combination of arches, its pressure has to be counteracted and neutralised by a well applied prop of masonry, and it is a feature that only appears in external medieval architecture. The buttress is indispensable where ribbed vaults are carried on fairly thin walls and is a development from the half-pier which terminates an arcade, or supports the impost of an arch springing away from a wall face. The first buttresses were responds protruding outwards from the external face of the wall against which an arch was thrusting. At first the buttress had a fixed dimension throughout its entire height, but later was given a greater projection at its lower courses and changes in the face were achieved by weathered 'set-offs'. Gables at the top of the buttress were subsequently superseded by pinnacles (Fig. 1.30), which were not just decorative but were used as a weighting device.

When buttresses were first used in the thirteenth century they were set out in pairs at the angles and matched those at the sides of the building. The practical experience of the masons made it apparent that unseen forces were at work and one of the chief problems was to counteract securely the thrusts of central nave or quire vaults springing from somewhere in the clerestory walls. They constantly tended to push outwards – a danger which intensified as the clerestory and vaults were increased in height. As it was impractical to bring the heavy buttress to earth through the aisle walls without seriously obstructing the floors, the thrust was consequently transmitted across and above the aisle wall by an inclined bar above an arch-segment – in effect, a tilted stone bridge which was incorporated into the top of a reinforced aisle buttress.

The flying buttress or flying arch is a system carrying the thrust of a roof or vault towards an isolated buttress. The designers realised that a flying buttress must have its flyer set at the most acute angle possible and that it must be set against the clerestory outside the vault springing. The curved part must be a fairly flat segment because the more it approaches a semi-circle the more likely it is to buckle. In some cases the 'flying piece' is channelled to function as a gutter, at the end of which a gargoyle – through which water discharges – projects from the pinnacle. This had certain drawbacks because the flying buttress was some way down the clerestory and rainwater had to be conducted down from the eaves.

Natural lighting was an important feature confronting the builders of this period, and was something that could not be solved effectively until the difficulties of vaulting and abutment had been overcome. It was not until the close of the twelfth century that the rows of deepset round-headed windows (Fig. 2.23) of the Anglo-Norman period began to be replaced by the larger pointed lancets which, arranged singly or in groups, lend such character to the façade design of thirteenth century English architecture.

**Fig. 2.23** Deepset round-headed window

**Fig. 2.24** Lancet

The new type of window which evolved matched the pointed arches of pier-arcades and vaults, and they had two distinctive forms. The window initially tended to develop in width rather than height, or remained narrow but increased in height. Where the window was broad and low it generally remained single, which gave the glass-painter great scope for design. Structurally, however, there were difficulties. Although the window had a polychrome beauty, it also had a wider surface to expose to wind pressure, which at first, until the introduction of stone mullions, could only be counteracted by a clumsy framework of iron bars. Where the window was narrow and tall it was soon grouped with other lancets (Fig. 2.24), often in threes, of which the central light was the largest; and in some cases all three were placed under a common dripstone. In other cases a group of lancets might be resolved into a single composition by being set in arcading, or by joining the dripstones into a continuous moulding.

The innovation of grouped lancets added a great deal to the façade design of transeptal churches due to the light that could be obtained from all four end walls in addition to the flanks. During the Anglo-Norman phase the simplest form of fenestration for end walls had

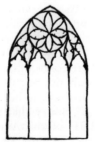

**Fig. 2.25** Traceried end-window

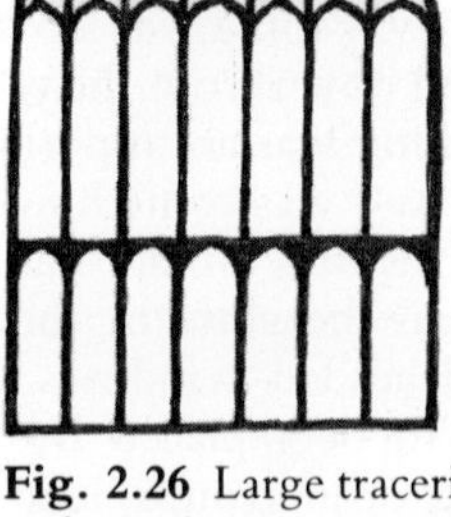

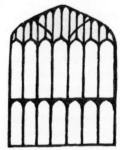

**Fig. 2.26** Large traceried end-window with many lights

**Fig. 2.27** Clerestory windows

**Fig. 2.28** Triforium chamber

continued for some time after the introduction of the lancets, but developed at the next step which threw the two lower tiers into one, giving an enormous increase in the volume of light. This paved the way for the introduction of the large traceried end-window of many lights (Fig. 2.25) and was to go a long way towards satisfying the medieval ideal of a building: a stone skeleton supporting the variegated expanses of its glazed walls (Fig. 2.26).

Side-lighting was achieved by the use of aisle windows and clerestory windows (Fig. 2.27), and as this latter system of top-lighting was often preferred and given precedence, a larger clerestory had to be provided.

When lower lighting from the aisles was required, the aisle walls

**Fig. 2.29** Grouped lancets

**Fig. 2.30** Plate tracery

were built high so that windows could be made larger. During this earlier phase another source of side-lighting was used in the form of borrowed light from the triforium, and in this case the aisle walls would be built high to incorporate a second range of windows to light the triforium chamber (Fig. 2.28) and therefore, indirectly, the nave. This had considerable influence on the internal bay design of Anglo-Norman churches and it demanded the opening out of the arcaded triforium – in extreme cases into a series of cavernous arches following the width of the pier arches below. The triforium window eventually disappeared from larger churches because of three external objections: the added expense of heightening the aisle walls; the necessary curtailment of the clerestory at the expense of a lofty triforium; and the fact that if the triforium windows were filled with stained glass, its effect was invisible from the body of the church, which was a pity because stained glass was then very popular.

The natural lighting of churches until the Early English phase was by grouped lancets (Fig. 2.29) which foreshadowed the mullioned and traceried window of the later Middle Ages. Nevertheless, the lancet form itself – tall and slender, with its beautiful combination of anything from two to seven lights – remained popular enough to be retained in England for a generation after it had been replaced in France, even though the evolution of tracery had proceeded steadily in the triforium. From the Norman period the arcades of this feature were made up of smaller arches beneath larger containing ones, and it was possible for the spandrels to remain solid. There was no difficulty in piercing them with circles, trefoils or quatrefoils and producing a simple form of plate tracery, as was the case in certain instances about 1118. At the beginning of the thirteenth century, plate tracery (Fig. 2.30) had become an almost regular feature of triforium design; the fenestration, however, remained unaffected for quite some time with the builders retaining their narrow lancet windows, possibly because it gave greater security to the stained glass.

A group of lancets set under a common dripstone probably provided the first incentive to produce a traceried window. The moulded stone mullions began to replace the iron bar to provide vertical support; the horizontal stone transom was not introduced until a later date. There were opportunities for developing the large window of many lights, strengthened with mullions and webbed at its head with an appropriate stone tracery that reflected the decorative ideals and advancing technique of the builders of each age. Between 1240 and 1315 plate or pierced tracery was gradually replaced by bar tracery built up of separate pieces of stone, geometrically simple, mainly in the shape of cusped circles. After 1280 other forms came into use such as the quatrefoil and trefoil: a centre-piece was often introduced in the form of a circle which would be filled with trefoils, quatrefoils and other designs (Fig. 2.31).

Circular windows filled with tracery were probably designed before oblong ones, and were known in the twelfth century – the favourite design being similar to a wheel with ornamental spokes which radiated from a central eye. It is not difficult to appreciate that if such windows were built to surmount a group of two or more lancets, the idea of an oblong window with traceried head would automatically arise. Later, the circular windows took much more elaborated forms following the designs of contemporary tracery. Triangular windows, or windows in the form of quatrefoils or other shapes, were also built to fill special positions, such as in the heads of gables (Fig. 2.32).

**Fig. 2.31** Trefoils and quatrefoils

**Fig. 2.32** Triangular windows in heads of gables

**Fig. 2.33**
Ogee curves

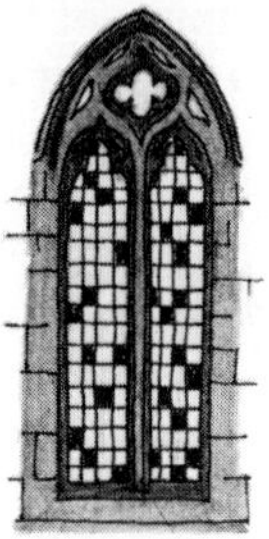

**Fig. 2.34**
Reticulated form

**Fig. 2.35**
Curvilinear tracery

The builders of the fourteenth century began to dispense with the rather formal geometrical shapes, partly due to the fact that they proved difficult for the glazier. Ogee curves (Fig. 2.33) were introduced, and because they appeared to blend into each other they were less obtrusive and natural and departed from the rigidity of the drawing board – in other words the tracery, though formal and using familiar geometrical shapes, became a complete flow of curves. Geometrical windows relied for beauty in their openings on circles, trefoils, quatrefoils and other shapes; decorated windows depended on the intricacy and beauty of the arrangements of the tracery bars. The 'reticulated' form (Fig. 2.34) was prevalent at this time and the window head was filled with repeating cusped ovals rather like the meshes of a net, but the overall effect was spoilt because the arch of the head cut the outer ovals into segments that were badly shaped.

Curvilinear tracery (Fig. 2.35) demonstrates the peak of the mason's skills in the church window, although his ability could be seen in the head tracery, especially when the window remained pointed. As the fifteenth century advanced, the containing arch tended to become flatter.

The windows in cathedrals and churches were always being enlarged during the medieval period, primarily to achieve more light but also to satisfy the desire for stained glass. The churches became stone lanterns with such windows, and although the tracery was mainly decorative it became a feature that enriched the buildings as a whole.

In the first paragraph of Chapter 1 reference is made to the towers and spires that come into view in town and country. Bell-towers (Fig. 2.36) had been in this country prior to the Norman Conquest, but there were few of them. Whether the tower is constructed of timber or stone, it signifies a considerable amount of skill in building during the medieval period; and it could be as expensive as the rest of the building yet only contain the bells. Some of these towers were at the west end, but this was not very convenient as the ground floor area which might be used was too distant from the main rituals

**Fig. 2.36** Bell tower

that took place at the other end of the building. Sometimes the tower was over the porch of the nave door, making it quite a feature, but it became unnecessarily large. Prior to the High Gothic period roofs were covered by several different methods, but during that phase flat lead roofs were the practice. One basic method was to build up to the opposite gable walls and place the roof as on any other building; another method was the Rhenish tower-top, built on four gables constructed by timbers joining their summits to form a diagonal square which carried rafters meeting to form a spire-like roof with four diamond-shaped planes (Fig. 2.37). It is most likely that the tower roof was originally constructed with rafters laid at a steep angle, and later the top of the tower was shaped like an octagon by having beams positioned across its angles. On this kind of base the rafters would have been set at a steep angle to form a 'broach' (Fig. 2.38) or spire which did not require transverse ties because there was no outward pressure. Four areas remained, each in the shape of a triangle; they were at angles of the tower and were covered by what can best be described as low lean-to roofs. These were covered by shingles and capped with a lead 'poll', which appears to have been a common covering for a roof of this kind as there are still some that remain in good condition. When lead was introduced as a roofing material it changed the construction because the base of the broach was formed by omitting the small roofs round the edge. The space remaining at each angle was covered with a lead flat and the corbel table, which was associated with the early eaves, was in most cases retained but was to have a parapet in future. This also applied to the rest of the church building.

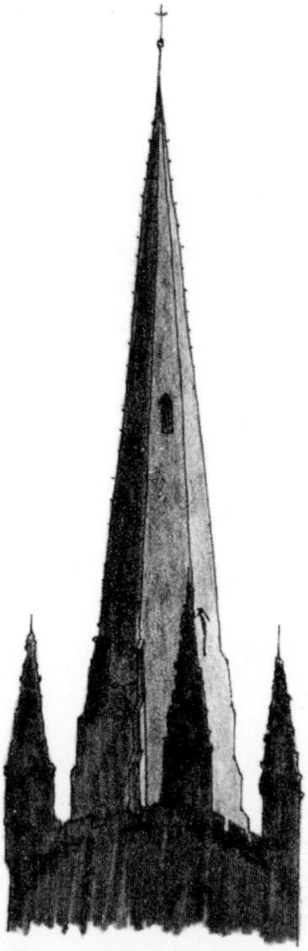

**Fig. 2.37** Spire roof

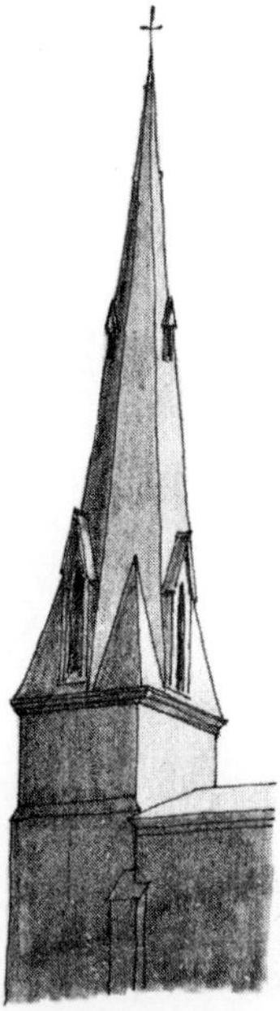

**Fig. 2.38** Broach steeple

**Fig. 2.39** Built-in staircase

**Fig. 2.40** Stair turret projection

The English masons now began to copy the timber angle-beams with squinch arches in stone, which was quite an achievement. Most of these towers had built-in staircases which gave access to the ringing floor (Fig. 2.39) and nearly all of them were worked into an angle. Different regions had their own characteristics, such as a stair turret projecting from the middle of a side wall (Fig. 2.40).

The elevations of large thirteenth-century towers were divided into bays by a medieval strip or a kind of buttress, and this continued into the High Gothic period. At belfry level the buttress divided this into two sections, each with a window, resulting in a most attractive architectural feature.

# *Chapter 3*
# Craftsmen and their achievements

Medieval craftsmanship took a considerable time to evolve and artistic achievement was rather isolated amongst a whole collection of crude and immature efforts, caused in some ways by unsettled governments, religious arguments and constant invasions. The Norman invasion did bring a certain equilibrium, the energy of which was expended on the erection of fortress-like churches, which were rather grim, due mainly to their austerity as there was an absence of ornament and decoration and little or no refinement. There were a few efforts to represent the human figure, but they were crude. Any attempt to decorate stone was done with a hatchet, and was confined to simple patterns surrounding doorways or arches leading into sanctuaries. At the beginning of the twelfth century there was a desire to furnish the churches with some degree of order and beauty, and some of the more enlightened clergy and nobles searched for talent. Craftsmanship was encouraged and a progression of the arts followed which lasted for nearly four hundred years. During this period craftsmen were under the patronage of the king and ecclesiastics.

The elements used by the craftsmen for the enrichment of the churches were surprisingly few in number, but adequate for the work they were expected to perform. The rendering was completely understood and, therefore, was rarely monotonous. In some ways ideas were limited and were used repeatedly in stone, timber, tiles, glass and other materials, but in each case the distinctive qualities were emphasised. It is convenient to divide the elements into architectural, natural and abstract. The architectural element consists of hollows and rounds applied to mouldings, shafts and tracery enriched with cusps, crockets and finials (see Fig. 1.28) which were taken directly from the construction of the building and adapted to ornamental purposes in the decoration. For example, capitals

**Fig. 3.1** Piscina

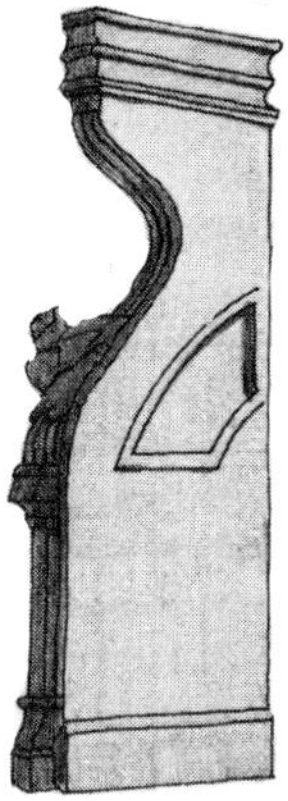

**Fig. 3.2**
Wooden stall

**Fig. 3.3**
Figurework

(Fig. 1.23), vaulting, rib and tracery were used with magnificent effect as the principal ingredients of a cathedral and applied with great success to a small niche. The gable is quite satisfactory in the termination of a large church, the finish to a canopied tomb, or in the decoration of a small piscina (Fig. 3.1). Buttresses and pinnacles were transferred from the exterior to the interior reproduced in miniature and made relevant to their new positions. In this work the craftsmen enjoyed adapting such elements to their designs, be it the reredos or wooden stalls (Fig. 3.2).

Nature was responsible for inspiring another type of design consisting of flowers, insects, foliage and sometimes animals, together with a good deal of figurework (Fig. 3.3). This does not mean that nature was carefully copied; the craftsmen, however, were able to achieve very successful representations of things they saw around them. Abstract forms were used in coats of arms, badges (Fig. 3.4) and monograms. Most of their ideas of proportion fell into two classes: architectural and symbolic. The architectural aspect was the figure sculpture of the façades and porches of the ecclesiastical buildings, and the symbolic proportions were determined by the relative importance of the object to person portrayed (Fig. 3.5). There was also a sense of humour, considered by some to be indecent. It must be remembered that in the craftsmen's day justice was not impartial and judgement was often given with flippancy and jest.

We have had stone buildings since prehistoric time, but this must not be confused with skilled masonry. In early days it was the practice to clear a site by moving the stones to the edge so that a heap was formed in some kind of rough wall which eventually was used

**Fig. 3.4**
Monogram

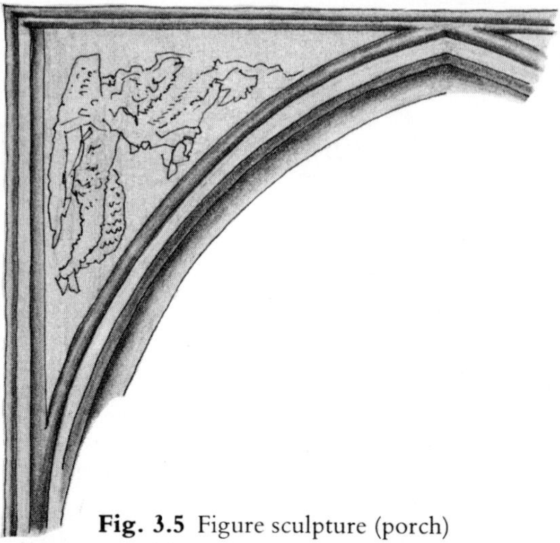

**Fig. 3.5** Figure sculpture (porch)

to form the walls of buildings; this technique became known as random rubble (Fig. 3.6). Many parish churches were built in this manner, not by masons but by wallers or 'nobblers' using hammers. There is nothing wrong with this kind of wall provided that mortar is available for bedding the stones; however, it was discovered that this type of wall had limitations. Unless properly 'dressed' stones were used for lining openings and reinforcing angles, crumbling could occur – creating an obvious weakness. Good quoins or angle stones are essential to the stability of a wall, and from this masons learned the craft of constructing a masonry wall (Fig. 3.7). The wall we are considering here has two faces, the space between being filled with core material (Fig. 3.8). About the middle of the medieval period, the core was made of carefully laid stones, which reduced the thickness of the walls.

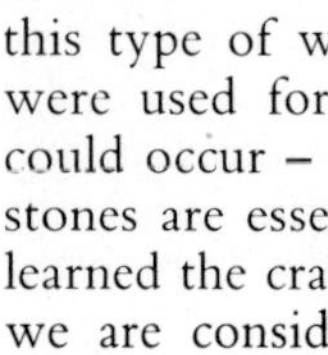

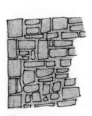

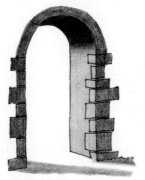

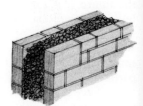

**Fig. 3.6**
Random rubble

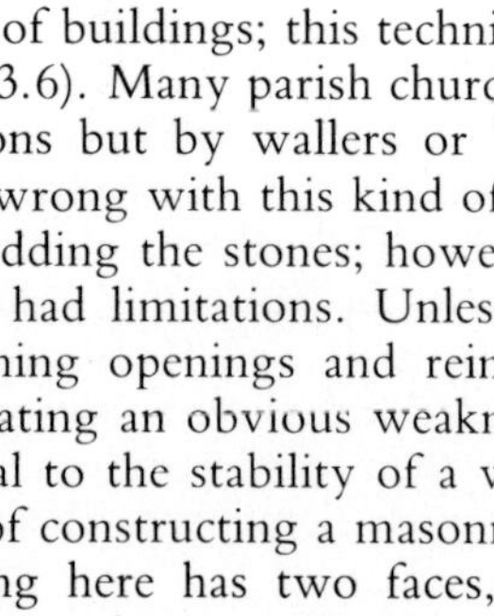

**Fig. 3.7** Quoins

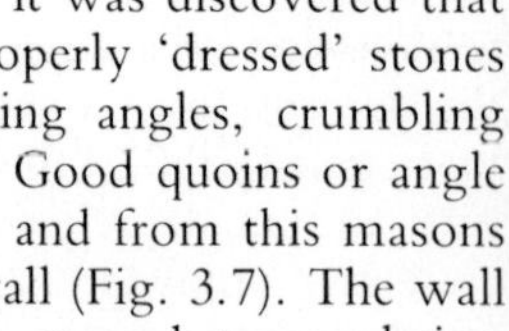

**Fig. 3.8** Core

**Fig. 3.9** Tomb

In masonry each stone has a 'face' and two 'beds', one on which to lie and one to carry the stone above. The face is squared to meet the stones on each side, and the remainder of the stone, i.e. the part hidden in the wall, is called the 'tail'. The mason cut his stones with the aid of an L-shaped iron called a 'square' on which his measurements were marked, and to obtain his curves on mouldings he had what we now call dividers. To identify his work, every mason had his own 'mark' which was not intended to be seen and was usually found on the 'bed' of the stone. The mason would have the job of explaining the complicated features to clients by the use of models, and mouldings would be cut out of lead sheet or board to form a 'template'.

An essential partner of the stone mason was the stone carver, whose ideas mainly evolved from the buildings on which he worked. He used various architectural features to produce his own decorative values, and quite apart from figure and foliage sculpture, he was successful in the bases, columns and capitals, arcades and buttresses canopies and nichework that were used in designing chantries, reredoses, sedilias, shrines and tombs (Fig. 3.9).

Until the twelfth century carving was rough and crude. When ornament first appeared it was cut with a hatchet, which was not a refined tool. Before the middle of the century a great deal of progress had been made; enriched mouldings were numerous, and when seen round the head of doorways they formed a rich pattern. The chevron (Figs. 1.2 and 1.4) was usually the basis for the design, but the lozenge, disk, chain, cable or beak were also used (Fig. 3.10).

(a) lozenge

(b) cable

(c) beak

**Fig. 3.10**

**Fig. 3.11** Tympanum

When churches were rebuilt in the twelfth century, doorways were often preserved, of which some very fine examples remain. In this period the inner semi-circular heads were cut in the solid and the tympanum was carved with symbolic subjects (Fig. 3.11), but it was rather poor work of feeble design. Figure sculpture had little quality until the beginning of the thirteenth century.

During the middle of the twelfth century the decoration applied to the portals was splendid, and replaced all that was lacking in earlier designs. Mouldings were enriched with medallions that had figure subjects, signs of the zodiac, beasts and birds (Fig. 3.12). These same mouldings were applied to chancel arches and, in some cases, main arcades.

A major asset of this period was the wall arcade – used extensively for exterior decoration – which can be seen on west fronts, (Fig. 3.13), towers, porches, turrets, on aisle walls, and inside porches, chapter houses, chancels, east ends and fonts. The stone-carver left a great deal of evidence of his craft in his work on fonts, large numbers of which remain, representing every type of shape: circular, square, and a slight variation of each (Fig. 3.14). The earliest fonts did not have a stem but were squat and usually bowl-shaped (Fig. 3.15).

Architectural features of the thirteenth century were the vertical lines of the shaft, gable and window. In the following century these features were broadened as well as enriched and the ogee arches were cusped, with spandrels filled with foliage and figure carving (Fig. 3.16).

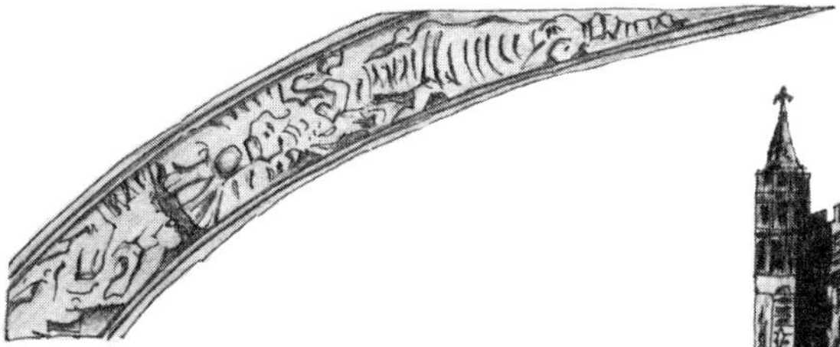

**Fig. 3.12** Beasts

**Fig. 3.13** West front

**Fig. 3.14** Font

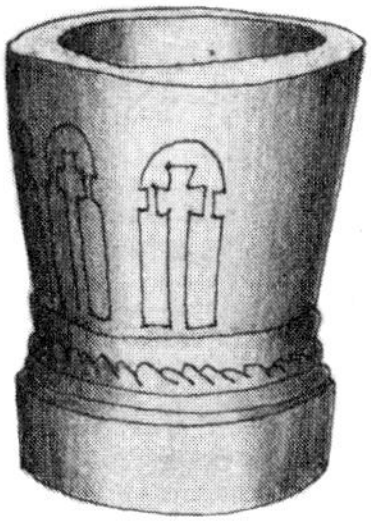

**Fig. 3.15** Squat and bowl-shaped font

For two centuries there was a trend for horizontal line which, till the end of the fifteenth century, became more accentuated in tomb and stallwork design. The horizontal line and closely ranged niche-work are the principal features of the fifteenth-century design found in the majority of porches, and are usually slightly cambered if they do not have a flat crown (Fig. 3.17).

Nichework, blind tracery and pinnacles are the chief sources of design in this period and form the decorative features. The masons and carvers of the early medieval period endeavoured to replace the crude efforts of previous years with work that was delicate and refined.

Medieval sculpture differed from that of the Greeks and Romans, and in the thirteenth and fourteenth centuries there was a number of masons who were able to carve or produce excellent sculpture. Most

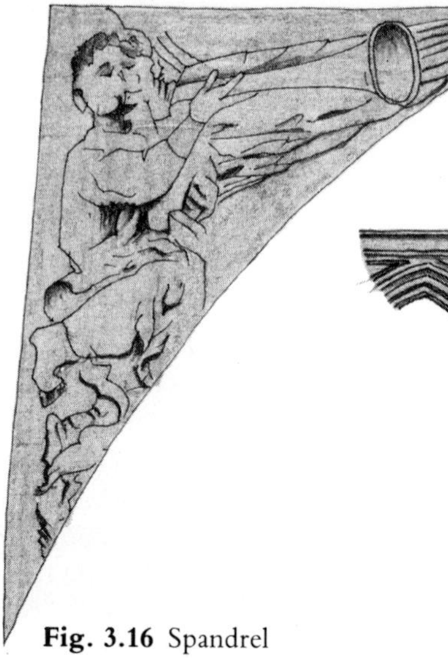

**Fig. 3.16** Spandrel

**Fig. 3.17** Nichework

of the medieval figurework was carved in coarse freestone and was homogeneous with the architecture it decorated. From a reading of ancient documents and a study of cathedrals and churches it is apparent that from the thirteenth century onwards figure sculpture was the crowning feature of the interior and exterior of these buildings. Figure sculpture reflects the architecture of the latter part of the medieval period; the important work was not carried out in the mason's yard but at centres in different parts of the country, to be delivered where required.

Owing to the enormous output compared with other craftsmen of this period, it is commonly held that the figure sculptor performed his art in the thirteenth century, the stone-carver in the fourteenth century, and the carpenter and wood carver in the fifteenth century. Until this time the wood carver had failed to make sufficient demands on his material, partly because of the dominance of the mason. He used timber as stone and failed to realise the qualities inherent in wood; he dowelled his work, not even grasping the value of mortise and tenon. Not a great deal of early work remains, but where it is found it demonstrates a clumsiness in method compared to the later genius. The decorative sources were the simple arcade or trefoil found on tombs, screens and chests (Fig. 3.18).

There are indications – such as screenwork cut out of heavy planking – that woodworking in the thirteenth century was greatly under the influence of the mason. As the fourteenth century advanced woodworkers and wood carvers attempted ambitious ideas by interpreting stone achievements in wood. They were extremely ingenious but

**Fig. 3.18** Chest

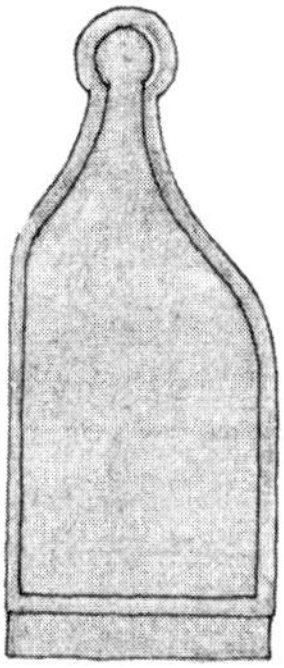

**Fig. 3.19**
Bench end

totally uneconomic, and it all ended in a wealth of material in the shape of flamboyant tracery in the heads of ogee arches and flowing tracery in each tapering gable. Wherever a surface offered opportunity the carver enriched it with tracery that was seldom duplicated. Natural foliage ran along the upper edge of each ogee and gable, and the gables and pinnacles were completed with knops of leaves.

The woodworker established himself in 1370; he was no longer subordinate to the mason but still applied his formulae. Although his application was different it was delicate and light, and he used the grain to advantage. His skill was displayed in the construction of roofs, the decoration on doors and porches, and on furniture, screens and stalls – especially if they had a canopy. Bench-ends – some with poppy-heads and some without (Fig. 3.19) – were a feature of the wood-worker. There is a diversity of design and shape, and as this was usually determined by the district the mouldings and carvings are endless: they could be bizarre, or charming, coarse or refined, rough or delicate, depending on the mood of the carver and the amount of work he had to do. Every kind of motif was used: tracery, figures, nichework, coats of arms, inscriptions, foliage, and merely plain ends. Apart from stalls, screenwork was the main output of the fifteenth-century craftsmen; the main screen included a rood-loft floor which was fenced on either side by gallery fronts decorated in a variety of patterns (Fig. 3.20). Beneath the floor of the loft was a cove or soffit; later, a lierne or fan vault. The proportions of these screens varied in different parts of the country and were determined in the execution of the design. The canopied spire, pinnacled and cusped, was used on font covers and pulpit testers as well as being the main feature of stallwork. The erection of a screen could take some time; the timber to be used was bought in the forest, felled and seasoned. Most of the work was executed in English oak although certain timbers were imported from overseas.

The carpenters were indispensable craftsmen who created remark-

**Fig. 3.20** Rood screen

able timber roofs, and no other country can excel more in design and construction. Many of these roofs are intact and can be seen throughout the British Isles. We remind ourselves of the types: the hammer, the beam, the arch brace, the first two being perfected in the fifteenth century (Fig. 3.21). The panelled beam roofs of the clerestoried period were enriched by deep mouldings and decorated with carved bosses and crow's feet; many of them were decorated with angels.

Glazing and stained glass (properly called painted glass) is of the twelfth century, although it was first used in England in 680. The early windows were composed of small pieces of glass which had to be cut to shape by a glazing iron; this was a tedious method and was extravagant in time. The glass had imperfections; it was uneven and thick, and as the chemical components varied they almost accidentally produced a richness. Windows with a theme were not attempted at first, and did not appear in England until 1170. There are limited remains of twelfth century glass in this country. The figurework of this period was not well drawn – hands and feet were badly proportioned – but there was a successful visual effect which resulted in a

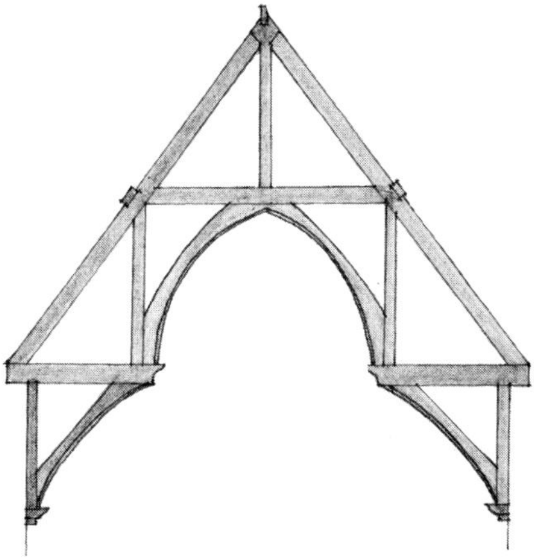

(a) arch brace

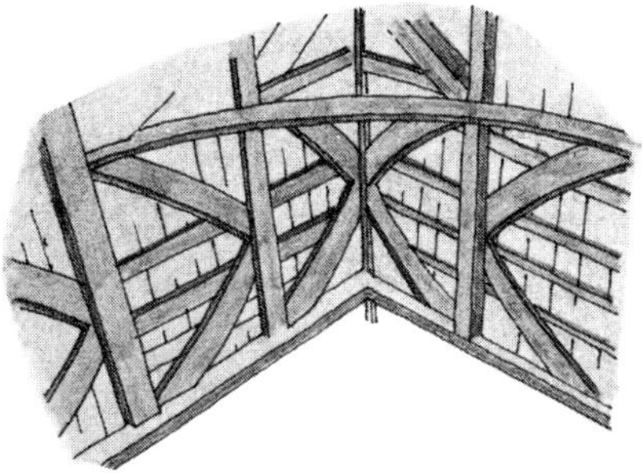

(b) hammer-beam

**Fig. 3.21**

glorious mosaic colour, mainly blue, green, ruby, maroon and 'pot-meal' (i.e. glass coloured in the melting pot). About 1280 the earlier forms of single figures and medallions were continued; the drawing had more finesse and the stain was not as deep. Flesh, which had previously been darkish brown in colour, now became a pinkish-brown hue.

Although this type of window was colourful it impeded the admission of light because of the intensity of the staining. A new window was developed which became known as grisaille (patterned). This was made of a grey coloured glass that had a tinge of green; it contained patterns of geometrical design, the background being either cross-hatched or unpatterned. The designs were elaborate, and when coloured glass was introduced they became a profusion of colour. During the period 1280–1350 the lack of development of other materials was reflected in the advance in the use of glass; it became

**Fig. 3.22**
Glazing

**Fig. 3.23**
Stained glazing

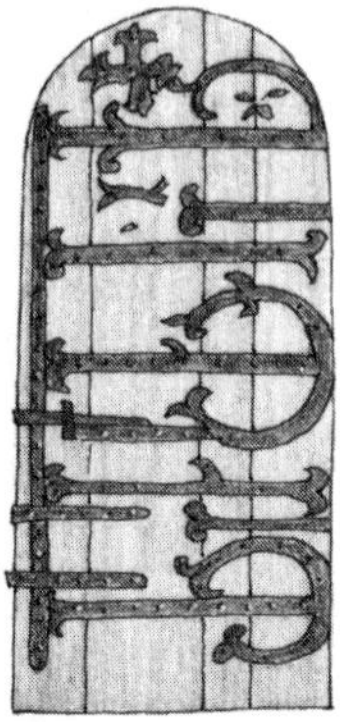

**Fig. 3.24**
Metalwork door

very popular, which encouraged the craftsmen to develop their ideas in design concept and glazing. As the technique progressed, larger pieces of glass were used (Fig. 3.22).

At the beginning of the fourteenth century the discovery of silver stain was to change the face and method of painted glass; and by the fifteenth century it had established itself among the other crafts. The windows of this period became a challenge to the glaziers; single lights had now become three or five, and as window tracery was more complicated they had to manoeuvre their figures and designs into the shape produced by the stonework, the province of the stonemason (Fig. 3.23).

In the fifteenth century glass entered its last phase, which in some ways was its finest. The canopy was the distinctive motif: greater use was made of white glass to frame the coloured figures; drawing was more refined; shading was stippled instead of smeared; and colouring became softer and not so intense. The subject panels depicted the lives of Christ, the Saints and the Virgin. The Crucifixion was drawn with simplicity and the Trinity was a popular subject.

The interior of a medieval church was ablaze with colour and not, as some suppose, watered down to an ecclesiastical half-tone as witnessed in so many 'colour schemes' of the present day. The colour, with the exception of white (an off-white), was applied in its brightest and purest form, each colour being separated from another by a fillet of white or gold. The carved portion was mainly gilded and was usually set against a blue background, although red and green were used alternatively in tracery, one for the face and the other for the hollows although sometimes red and blue were used. Such a system was probably prompted by the use of heraldic motifs in decorative carving. It was the intention of the medieval craftsman that his work, whether wood or stone, would ultimately be coloured. Walls were rendered with a thin layer of plaster to form a base for the paintings which were extremely varied in their composition. The scenes were not all religious; in fact, in numerous cases they had no resemblance to the Christian faith. Oil paint was the usual medium and was applied quite thinly. A type of tempera was used (not egg-based) which had a fish-glue basis. Several coats of white were applied to form a base for the composition and the fluid mixture of paint was rendered in small quantities to produce an even surface with no hint of brush marks and without hiding the mouldings. Very little of this style of painting remains in cathedrals, and what did exist has been covered by successive coats of plaster or has been scraped away during restorations, but many are still preserved in parish churches.

The craft of the metalworker included many varieties of work, from the massive to the minute and from the plain to the filigree of delicate loveliness. Medieval metalwork has largely disappeared, which is a tragic loss, but the little that remains enables us to admire and appreciate the craftsmanship. This is represented in the doors which had elaborate whorls and complicated twists (Fig. 3.24). The designs had various sources of origin; for example, swastikas and viking ships. Hinges were mainly crescent-shaped because they were considered to be strong and efficient. By the thirteenth century iron-work was fashioned in delicate vine growth; grilles and grates were very much a part of the ironworker's repertoire, used mainly for tombs and effigies (Fig. 3.25). His tools were simple: a hammer, anvil, fire and bellows. In the fourteenth century the smith changed his methods to meet new demands and treated his material not as a

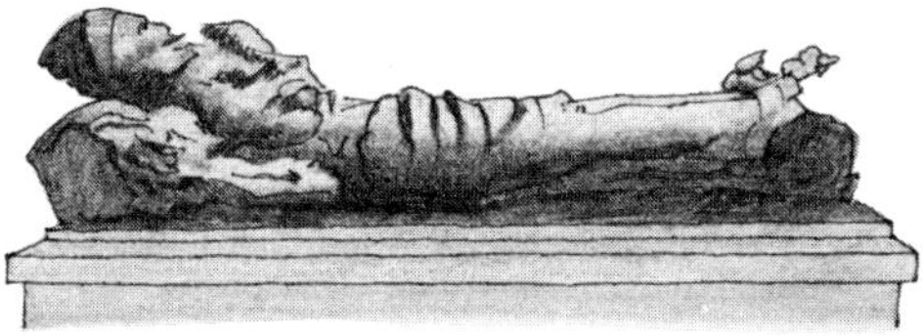

**Fig. 3.25** Effigy

**Fig. 3.26** Tiles

malleable metal but as timber, cutting and sawing it when it was cold.

Certain craftsmen of the twelfth century contributed their own skill in the form of tiles for floor coverings. These tiles were originally found in the sanctuary, chapter house, small chapels and other positions of dignity (Fig. 3.26), and they provided an enrichment; their colours were basically red, yellow, green and black but, owing to the impurities of the chemicals, there were some most attractive variations of tints. The sizes varied because the clay had a tendency to shrink when drying and baking. The finest periods of tile-making were in the thirteenth and fifteenth centuries; and tiles were usually made in the vicinity of the site. In the case of decorated or incised tiles, it was essential to situate the kiln near a bed of white clay which was necessary for the slip with which the designs were filled. The tiles were made by squeezing soft clay into wooden moulds that were usually square in shape with sloping sides. The clay was turned out while it was still pliable and a carved block of wood was impressed on the clay to give it a surface pattern. It was then left to dry, given a white slip which filled the hollows, left to dry again, and before firing in the kiln was sprinkled with lead ore which, when cool, gave the tile a metallic glaze – the red a richer tone and the white a yellowish hue. Manganese was used to colour the black tiles. Examples of these tiles remain throughout the country.

To appreciate fully the glory of the craftsmanship of the fifteenth century we have to exercise a vivid imagination by eliminating our present-held image of a church interior. Such an exercise would reveal a church interior that was harmonious in colour: the chancel separated from the nave by a screen beautifully carved with the gallery front painted with saints complemented by others in the stained glass windows and on the walls.

Where this has survived it must be cared for and preserved. It is a rich heritage and we are its custodians.

# *Chapter 4*
# Inspection and assessment

The previous chapters have briefly indicated the rich architectural heritage that prevails in Britain. Since the end of World War II there have been major problems and crises in the care and preservation of cathedrals and churches, which is a matter of considerable importance. Those responsible for the structure and fabric of such buildings have to decide why it is necessary to preserve them, and their decision will be based on historic, aesthetic or economic reasons, or perhaps all three. The care and preservation of ecclesiastical buildings implies maintenance, and maintenance in this context means regular inspection; this is essential because it will determine the priorities of work that can be programmed and suitably organised. The neglect of these buildings has a much wider implication than just depreciation of what survives. The cost of neglect is enormous.

One of the main sources of decay has water at its origin; it is the principal reason for organic, physical or chemical attack. Considering them briefly in this order we begin to appreciate why change takes place: an organic attack is made by the algae and lichens which, like all other vegetation, retain water. There are those who say that an aesthetically pleasing decay takes place in the colouring and texture produced by such growth. This is true, and can be visually attractive on buildings, but when neglected it can cause the structure to disintegrate. A tree can attack a building when it is adjacent because it shades a part of the building and prevents the drying effect of the wind and sun, encouraging the growth of fungus and moss (Fig. 4.1). The roots of a tree can penetrate walls and foundations by exerting great pressure, fracturing materials and opening joints. Ivy is a dangerous species since it supports itself by anchoring in the pores of mortar pointing (Fig. 4.2).

Timber can be the victim of fungal growth, encouraged by the

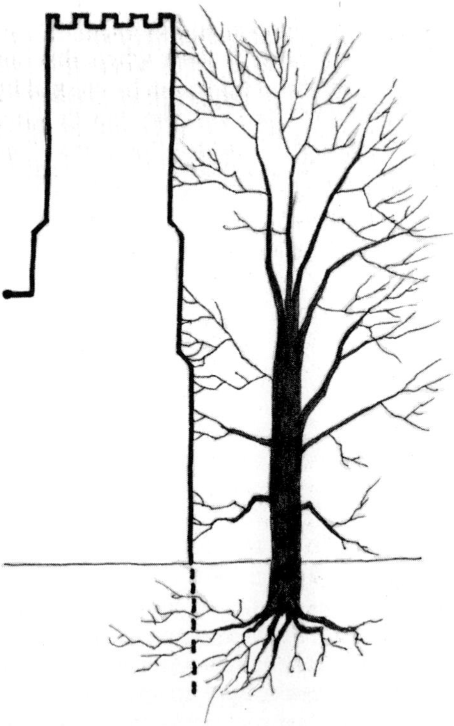

**Fig. 4.1** Tree attack

**Fig. 4.2** Ivy anchored in pointing

presence of moisture, causing serious decay. Fungal growth also has a deleterious effect on stone. Physical attack happens where water is allowed to penetrate the surface of a building through joints or porous surfaces, and when this happens the risk of frost damage is very real. The movement of a building caused by thermal stress, settlement or compression can be the indirect cause of decay, allowing the ingress of water through ruptures or open joints; but although ıis kind of damage can be sudden and dramatic, it can be remedied s it is visible. There is, however, a sense where this can be insidious: ıe slow opening of the cracks or joints can be masked by the accumu-.tion of dirt, and therefore the fault may not be obvious until the amage is extensive. The third consideration is the chemical attack in 'hich salts which are water-borne cause serious damage to the sur-.ce: for example, salts that are present in a material or are drawn 'om an adjacent material, such as soil migrating from the core by ıoisture movement. When this soil reaches the surface the water vaporates, leaving the salt as crystals which form efflorescence or, ıore dangerously, lie just below the surface which causes exfoli-:ion and consequent breakdown. Also, water soluble gases in the mosphere falling mainly in the rain (over which we have no con-ol) on surfaces can cause considerable damage due to the layers of ıemical deposits.

No medieval cathedral or church can be left to perpetuate its life 'ithout repair or restoration under specialist supervision. Restor-ion is not haphazard, and cannot be left to those who are content 'ith a patched-up job; it requires expertise that is not only techni-ılly sound but is generously sensitive to the architectural heritage. his need is underlined by the factors stated above which are a threat the type of buildings with which we are concerned. In addition, ıere are gradual activities which may react for a hundred or more ears before they are considered serious enough to justify attention: r example, the movement of foundations, changes in the under-'ound environment, erosion due to wind and rain, structural dam-ge to vibration, unsuitable forms of heating, and alterations to the ternal layout. Other factors which may occur in less time, but hich require attention, are condensation, rising damp, wood-ɔring beetle, the usual wear and tear of floors, doors and iron-.ongery, plus the damage that is caused by a lack of regular, basic, neral maintenance. It is still surprising that many ecclesiastical ımmunities do not appear to realise that careful maintenance can ɔntribute greatly to the postponement, and even the avoidance, of ıbstantial repairs. If they do, they fail to bring it to the attention of eir congregations and the public. In fairness, let it be said that this ıte of affairs has improved in recent years – especially where eccle-ıstical buildings are concerned.

It is essential that early inspection and assessment are organised to esent some kind of diagnosis before any action is taken. Many fac-rs have to be considered, because the damage could have been used by more than one agent, making the problem difficult to fine. This is where expert advice is necessary; a complete structural rvey is required before any major work is advocated. It is not an ıusual event and should happen when a survey of dilapidation takes ıce on any building; it is a routine procedure on more recent build-gs. In the case of medieval buildings which have complicated

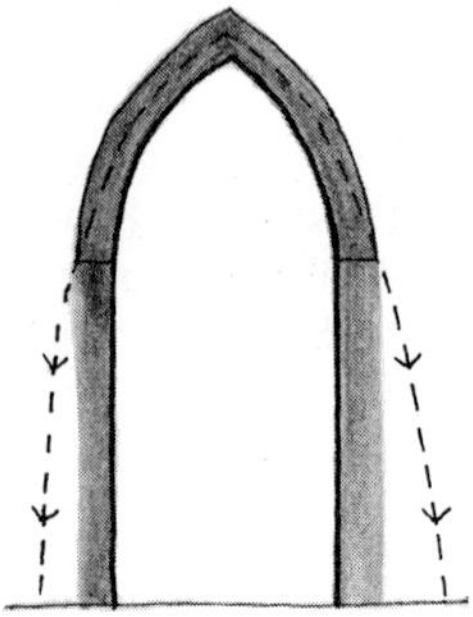

**Fig. 4.3** Thrust

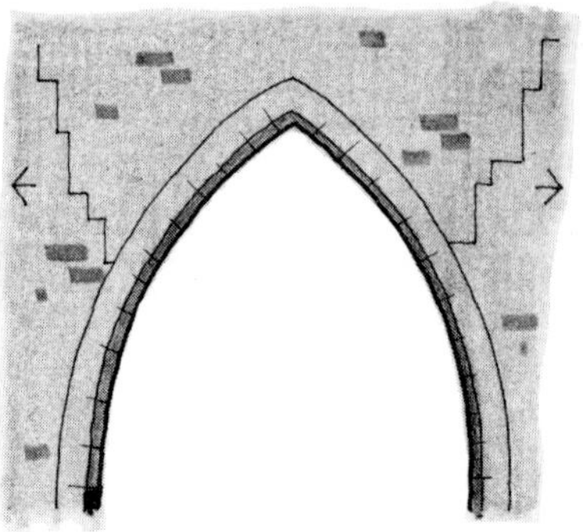

**Fig. 4.4** Cracked arched wall

Gothic structures, the survey has to be meticulous, dealing wit structural principles of thrust and counter-thrust where the variou forces at work have to be understood (Fig. 4.3). This kind of inve tigation must establish the forces that are at work in the structure ar determine the cause of structural failure. If defects are identified tl next question is: 'What are the consequences if the defects in tl structure are not rectified?' When an arch is cracked and its suppor are obviously leaning outwards, it usually means that somethir must be done to strengthen them to resist any continuing thrust the arch (Fig. 4.4). This is an obvious fault which can be dealt wit at once.

Before any major remedy can be considered on this part of th structure, there must be an intensive examination which can be tim consuming and can involve the inspection of the fabric stone b stone, requiring analysis, research and synthesis. These factors alo underline the importance of the architect knowing and understandir the fabric in detail both technically and aesthetically. The structur of a medieval building can be more highly stressed in some par than in others, but if there has been a variation in stress there can b distortion; the signs of crushing are more likely to be found in th piers under a tower than in the low walls surrounding a chapel. If wall is going to crack it will do so at its weakest point, which will b where it is broken by the largest opening or where it is thinnest. situations like these there has to be a means of measuring movemen such as the use of a 'tell-tale'. Other parts that the experienced e will observe are the junctions of walls and arcades, nave arcade pie opposite the west walls of transepts, and the sills of wide windov near ground level (Fig. 4.5).

Medieval buildings were liable to subside in their early years un they eventually found their own level. One of the facts resulti from this was the uneven compression of thick walls when the init weight of the superstructure rested. The rubble core had not settl and was unconsolidated; it found its level lower down, which w

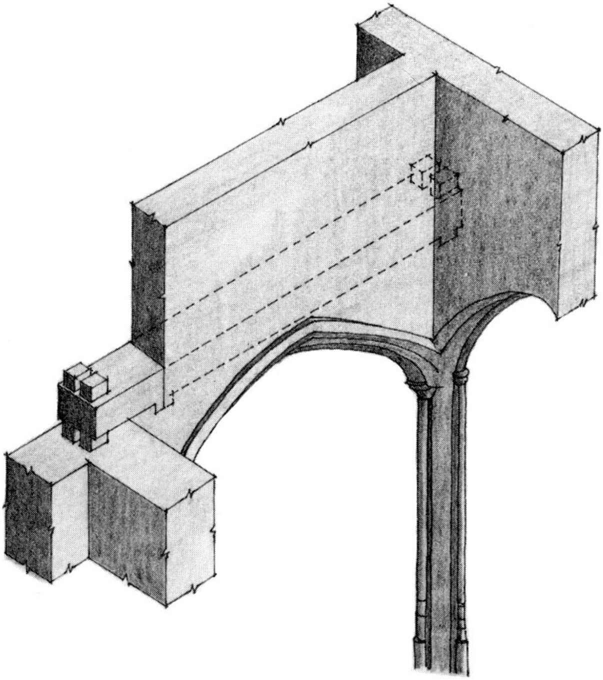

**Fig. 4.5** Junction of walls and arcades

rther than possible in relation to the adjoining ashlar. This meant at the stone had to take more than its share of weight, and often ctured. Allowing for the fact that these structures settled long ago d that there is certain evidence of stress, great care must be taken make sure that there is no cause for alarm. Where junctions of avy and light structures occur, cracks can be found; but this need t be viewed with dismay as long as the structure on both sides is ble. One of the structural features in cathedrals and churches is at junctions of vaults and walls – especially in medieval intersecting ults which are built on the principle that the weight of every part them is concentrated upon the supporting piers with the butsses. The safety in this method of building is such that the ult would remain intact if the walls between the main piers were molished. This also applied later in the period when the entire ll space below the vault and between the piers had windows.

Fractures may appear between the vault and the lateral wall and ll be seen at the line of the wall-rib where the vault appears to be ting on the wall (Fig. 4.6). This does not mean danger because the ult does not depend on the adjoining walls for support – at least t at this point. Any attempt to repair such a fracture by joining the ult and wall and making them rigid will cause disintegration in the

**Fig. 4.6** Fractures between vault and lateral wall

**Fig. 4.7** Staircase turret

structure and introduce a weakness in an otherwise structurally sa condition. This can be readily explained if we note that the su stantially thick wall remains in a reasonably stationary conditi throughout the changing temperature of the seasons, whereas a va is essentially a thin structure which reacts quickly to changi temperature and is also shaped in such a way that any expansion tl occurs must move towards the apex. If it is going to remain health it must be allowed to 'breathe'. Further fractures can take place b tween wood and masonry – that is, beams, frames or posts and t masonry and plaster which cover them – and will occur in most ca as a result of humidity rather than structural movement because t builders of the medieval period finished their plaster and mason flush with the surface of the wood. Tower staircases were usua circular on plan and were built in half the thickness of the main w the other half being the external wall of the staircase turret. In tov staircases it is possible to find certain structural settlements in surrounding walls (Fig. 4.7). The outer skin of masonry of the tov is much thinner than the inner skin, being only one stone thick. T inner wall will have the usual rubble core while the outer wall for part of the arc of a circle and is tied together by the radiating sto of the staircase.

The foundation of any building is the base on which it rests. purpose is to distribute the load safely to a suitable subsoil. T foundation of medieval buildings often failed in the first years af erection, but subsequently ceased to move many years ago. It therefore, necessary to remember that such buildings can move co siderably before they became dangerous. Part of the explanation this is that the ground has become fully compressed and that me eval walls were thick. There is a sense where buildings of this age naturally stand up. If this is regarded with some suspicion, a look at some medieval ruins will demonstrate how masonry will stand upright in spite of centuries of exposure to the elements.

It is necessary to distinguish a defect in the foundation from one which is confined to the superstructure. The defects are interdependent and both can produce similar fractures above ground level: if the superstructure is inadequately designed, and the weight is unevenly distributed, there can be foundational failure. If the load is even in its distribution the foundations may not require strengthening. The greatest movement is high up to the elasticity in most medieval buildings and, being so, it can absorb any small movements at a lower level. If it is established that the movement is foundational, the whole area must be explored as deeply as possible. Arches and roofs that are not tied never cease to spread outwards, and if this kind of pressure is the cause of a foundation problem then the situation can become serious. In medieval buildings, however, this will only become a threat if new factors are introduced – some of which can be caused by various kinds of excavations nearby, such as new roads and graves. It is essential that these possibilities are fully explored and understood otherwise needless underpinning may take place at great expense which will not necessarily eliminate the weakness that had caused the failure. Boreholes (Fig. 4.8) may be required if hand-dug trial holes prove fruitless.

Having determined the cause of movement in the foundation and decided on the best method to bring it to a point of stability, it is then sensible to consolidate the superstructure before starting the underpinning.

There are numerous other threats to medieval cathedrals and churches, some of which are slow-acting and may take many years to become serious enough to demand repair – for example, thermal movements, changes in the underground environment, erosion due to rain and wind, structural damage due to vibration, and unsuitable forms of heating.

Other factors that will take from five to thirty years to cause damage worthy of repair are rising damp, condensation, wood-boring beetle attack, normal wear and tear of floors, doors and ironmongery, and damage due to lack of regular painting. Threats that will act very quickly and cause not only visual but hidden damage are inadequate rainwater disposal or blocked drainage, leaking roofs and gutters. The decay of materials will cause changes in the stress distribution and loading. Certain faults due entirely to lack of basic maintenance can become apparent within a year; and there is also frost, overloading and the outbreak of dry-rot which can result from damp penetrating valleys, gutters and downpipes. All these are under the constant scrutiny of the architect in charge (sometimes called 'surveyor' when dealing with cathedrals) who has overall responsi-

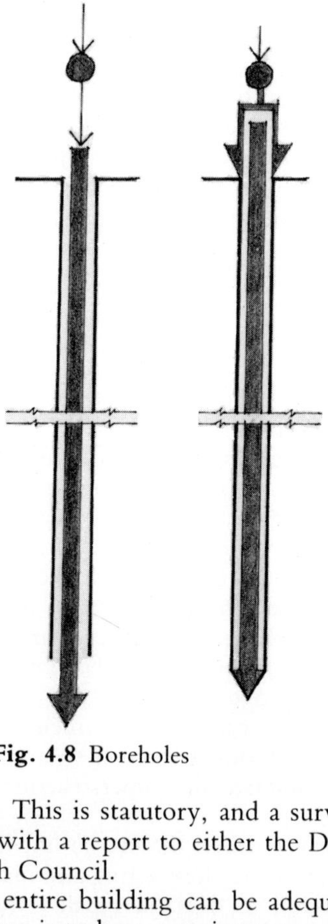

**Fig. 4.8** Boreholes

bility for the fabric. This is statutory, and a survey must take place at regular intervals with a report to either the Dean and Chapter or the Parochial Church Council.

In order that the entire building can be adequately cared for and preserved the first step is to have a maintenance plan, based on a detailed survey by the architect, which may indicate the need for structural repair. Depending on the requirements, the architect will assemble a team of specialists which would include consulting engineers, mechanical and electrical consultants, art historians, archaeologists, archivists and a quantity surveyor – the last being vital in the costing of the work in view of budgeting and financial appeals. The architect will co-ordinate the contribution of each of those mentioned and any other specialist who may be called, and he will need special knowledge of historic buildings (and how they age and decay), the preservation of materials, and special techniques used in the construction of medieval cathedrals and churches. Also, as conflicting values will arise to be resolved, it is essential that a knowledge of the history of the subject is obtained by those engaged in the work on the fabric in order to make decisions.

An initial inspection and assessment are important for whatever happens subsequently. As far as the structure and fabric are concerned, the medieval cathedral or church is a cultural document and, therefore, its integrity must be safeguarded and respected. The original design and material must be retained as much as possible; the architect is involved in making value judgements, and repairs should avoid disrupting the visual unity. Each cathedral and church must be assessed carefully against its architectural, historical and archaeological value and treated on its merits.

# *Chapter 5*
# Foundations, stonework and walls

It cannot be stressed too much or too often that prevention by regular inspection and maintenance is much more satisfactory in preserving cathedrals and churches than do-it-yourself, temporary repairs. There is occasionally the temptation to do a 'cosmetic' job, which can be satisfactory in some cases; however, it is more probable that the work will eventually have to be done thoroughly and it is therefore better to have the problem assessed early and dealt with by specialist craftspeople who know their subject and their materials.

Let us now deal in more detail with foundations. In certain cases the distance between the highest level or surface ground and the lowest solid course can be short, and these shallow layers of weakness can cause defects in the walls. The builders of the medieval period tended to be rather careless in the building of their foundations. It is known, for example, that they would take them down to levels which would be considered dangerous by present day requirements, standards and regulations. They laid them on ground that was soft and pliable instead of going slightly deeper, where the ground was probably solid. On the other hand if a solid base is desired at some depth below the surface, underpinning may be necessary, which can be quite expensive (Fig. 5.1).

Another available method involves inserting longitudinal beams under the walls and supporting them at intervals, which means that the structure is in fact standing on stilts (Fig. 5.2). Should the measurement in the vertical dimension be reasonable, the stilts can function as piers. A further method is the use of reinforced concrete piles, which are placed in such a way that each will bear an equal load (Fig. 5.3).

It is important to consider the situation when the ground is marshy and beyond the scope of normal foundations; the building,

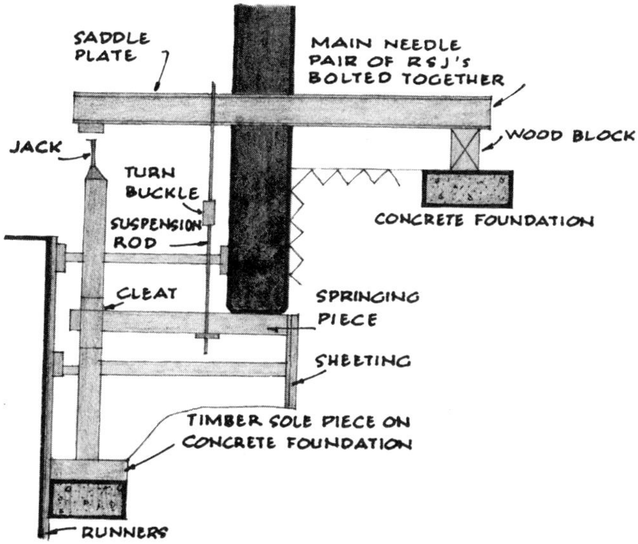


**Fig. 5.1** Underpinning

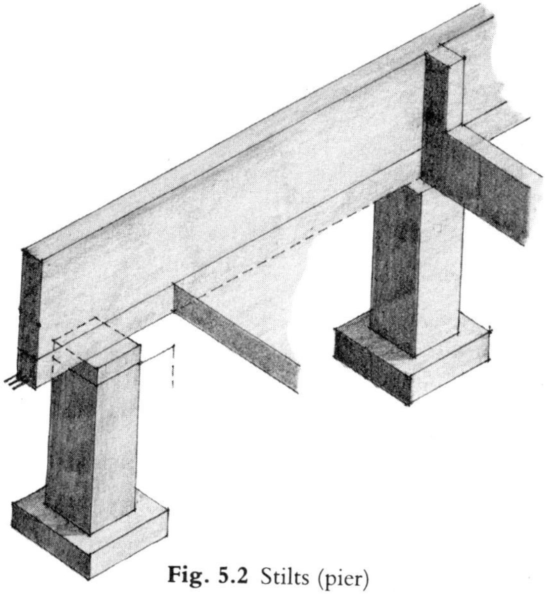

**Fig. 5.2** Stilts (pier)

in fact, is sinking! In this case the normal pile foundation is not adequate unless the soft wet ground is shallow enough to allow the piles to reach the solid bottom. A repair in this situation will probably require the 'raft' method which is strong enough to distribute the weight of the walls and piers evenly. The raft, however, must cover

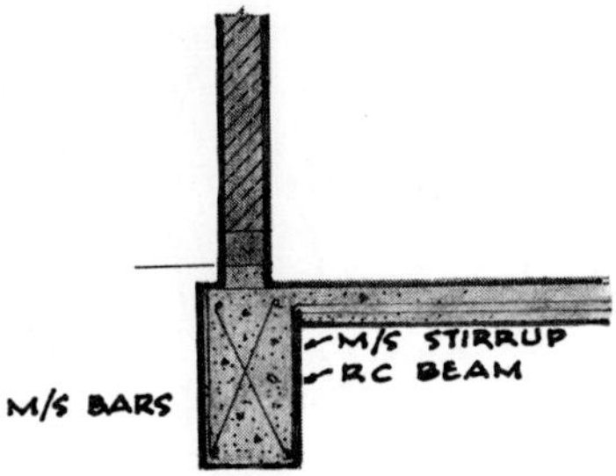


**Fig. 5.4** Raft

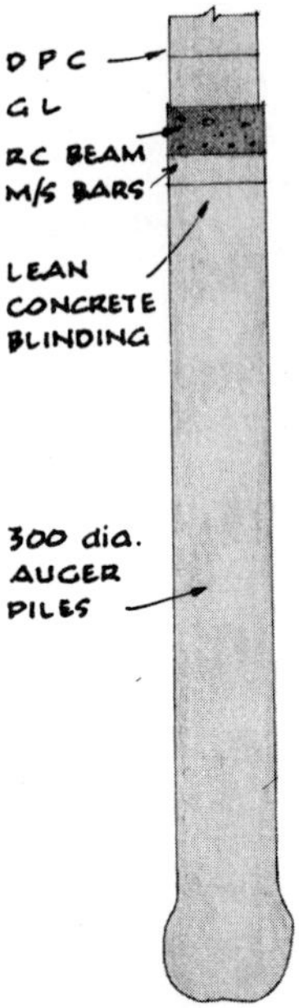


**Fig. 5.3** Concrete piles

the area of the whole building – that is, the entire building is literally afloat (Fig. 5.4).

In this type of operation a soil mechanic should first investigate the site, and in order to do this the main piers will have to be strapped before any excavation takes place. In this whole procedure a constant vigil will have to be maintained as burial chambers may be discovered at any level; and in fact the whole area being considered may be honeycombed, with the result that it is unable to provide much lateral restraint. The existing foundations must be measured and the soil excavated. The soil will be replaced by sandbags, and heavy planking and strutting will have to be inserted to enable the new foundations to be built. The existing material should be used where possible so that minimum disturbance occurs to the fabric, but the details of this aspect will be the responsibility of the experts. A careful watch will be required when the new foundations accept their load, and a further examination of the soil may also be necessary. Although many ecclesiastical buildings in the medieval period were built on a continuous waterproof raft, quite a number were 'floating' since the ground on which they were standing moved with each change in water level. These buildings were, in most cases, founded on timber beams and the timber may have decayed over the years.

Substantial structures require less depth in their foundations than lighter buildings because their weight counteracts expansive tendencies in the soil. This situation can be used to advantage in the case of underpinning on clay soil because, under certain parts, it may not be

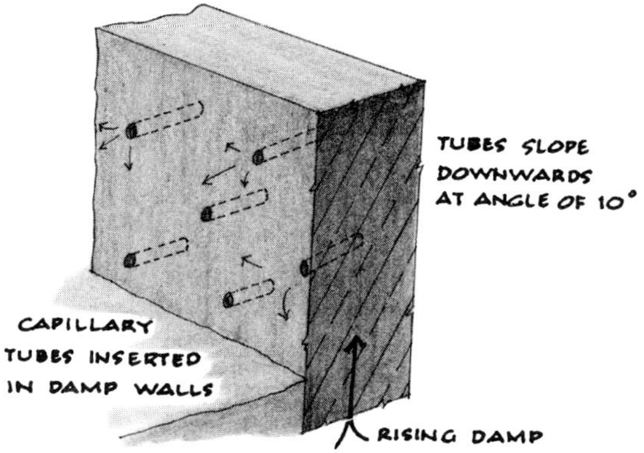


**Fig. 5.5** Damp

necessary to carry the foundations as deep as those elsewhere. If a wall is being underpinned, the opportunity should be taken to insert a damp-proof course as this is rarely found in medieval buildings. It would be wise not to use bitumen, for where there is lateral movement it is possible that one part of the wall will move across the other.

At this point it is necessary to draw attention to the matter of damp, which must be kept under control as much as possible. It is a most destructive agency and is a major contribution in reducing the physical life of materials, undermining their resistance to erosion and frost. It has an attraction for pests, it softens timber and is a breeding ground for fungal growth. A major factor in the care and preservation of cathedrals and churches is the constant control of natural moisture throughout the building. In order to deal with this problem it is necessary to locate its source, as dampness can originate from the ground, from humidity or from the elements – quite apart from any faulty plumbing that may exist (Fig. 5.5).

Moisture is a great traveller either by capillary action or by gravity; it will move towards any drying element such as warm or cool air currents, and it will also descend. It can be remedied by a counter-attraction or by the creation of a water-vapour barrier (Fig. 5.6). The best and most efficient cure is the provision of adequate ventilation (Fig. 5.7). The other aspect of this problem is rising damp, which can be a constant source of trouble in a wall without a damp-proof course, and occurs when moisture is attracted upwards by capillary action (Fig. 5.8). It does not travel alone, but is accompanied by soluble salts which cause damage to masonry and completely disfigure decorations. The only remedy for rising damp is to build in a damp-proof course, which is an expensive and major operation. There have been several traditional ways of doing this, one of which was to shore up and remove alternative sections of the lowest courses of walling and build in a course of slate or engineering brick. The re-

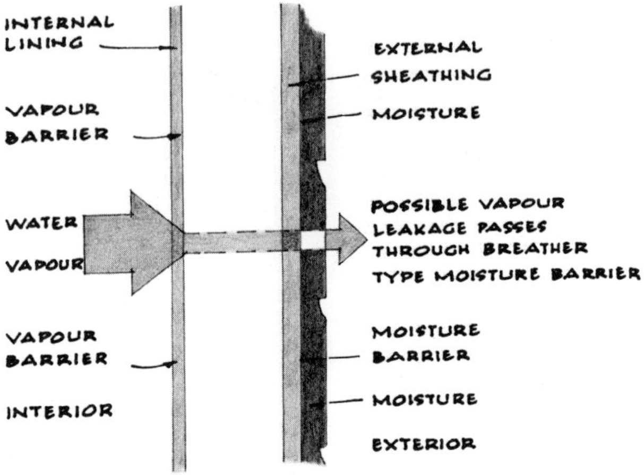


**Fig. 5.6** Vapour barriers

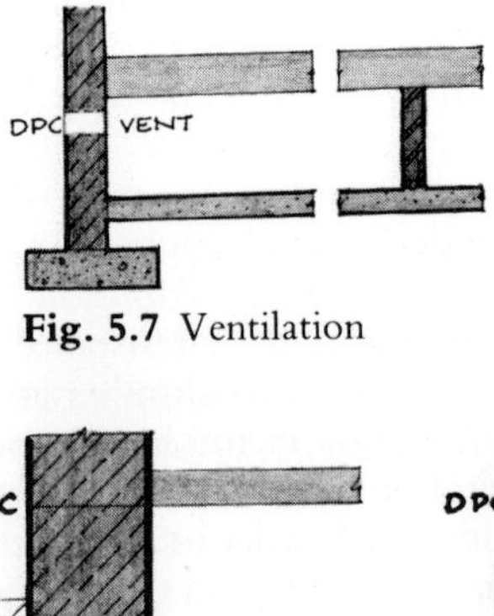


**Fig. 5.7** Ventilation

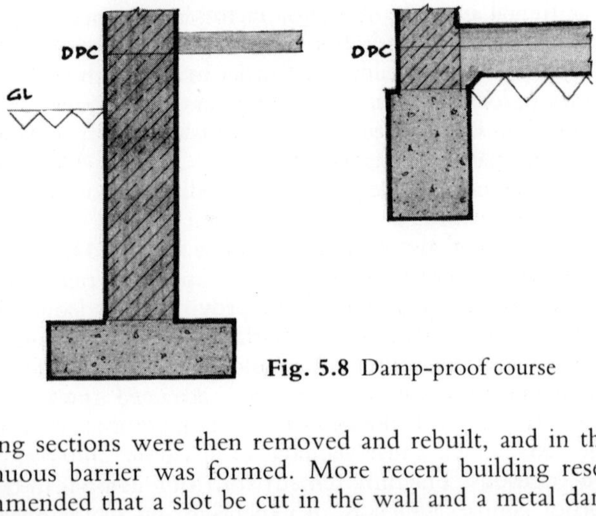


**Fig. 5.8** Damp-proof course

maining sections were then removed and rebuilt, and in this way a continuous barrier was formed. More recent building research has recommended that a slot be cut in the wall and a metal damp-proof membrane inserted in sections (Fig. 5.9).

The same principle for any damp-proof course will be applied in this situation and it should be at least 6 in (150 mm) above the exter-

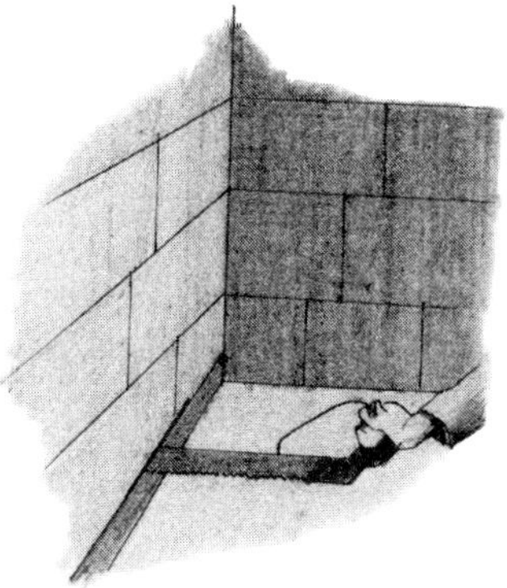

**Fig. 5.9** Sawing a slot

al ground level. If the cut can only be made above floor level, the ertical face of the wall between the new damp-proof course and the .oor should be treated with two coats of bituminous paint and the nembrane must be continuous.

The source of penetrating moisture is usually obvious, and de-ective roof valleys, gutters and rainwater pipes bring destruction o walls and other parts of the building. Few materials are totally npervious and most materials hold or carry moisture to some egree.

There are solutions to all these questions and problems and a num-er of products are available that can be applied to walls to form a rotective skin; one such solution is a mixture of equal proportions f petrol and linseed oil. There are others, developed from the sili-one water repellants, which repel moisture and at the same time do ot choke the pores. These solutions coat the walls with a water-epellant layer, making it possible for air to pass whilst the water is epelled and runs off the material. The silicone water repellants also iscourage the adhesion of dirt which may build up and disfigure the urface.

Looking at a medieval cathedral or church it is obvious that the nost predominant material is stone. We have considered the way in vhich these stones were worked to achieve an aesthetic result. Con-ideration must now be given to the possibility of stone decay. The noment a stone is put in position there are forces at work that try to ffect its efficiency, and one of the first things to look for is a defect n the stone itself. It is also possible that it may not have been quar-ied correctly or it may have been laid wrongly or set in non-porous ointing. It could also be due to different kinds of stones being laid ogether. Frost can have a serious effect on stone; expanded water nay have penetrated which will cause crazing and, eventually, de-omposition. Certain kinds of salt can enter the stone from the mor-ar and/or the soil. In addition, there is the ever-present danger of pollution by acids. It is difficult to appreciate that soot can caus many problems. Aircraft discharge enormous quantities of pollutio and drop-out which settle over a very wide area forming a hard sur face – a skin that manifests itself in various ways with serious conse quences. The problem is, that the breakdown is taking place withi the stone and is not visible until the stone powders and cracks.

What cure can be prescribed for this problem? Numerous first-ai repairs have been attempted over the years, and some of them hav caused extensive damage to the stone through the misguided use c chemicals – in many cases the more haste the less speed, or a littl learning is a dangerous thing, or perhaps both! Preservatives hav been introduced, and other resins have been added to the silicon o the silicon has been considerably chemically modified. The preserv atives that are silicon based are liquids which easily penetrate the ston and develop into a gelable consistency. The preservative, therefore does not spread and the completion of the curing process to form th final product takes place in the layer of the stone that has been pen etrated up to that point. The formulations vary according to th period that elapses between the initial mixing and the commence ment of gelling, and also to the rate of change from liquid to gel.

This is a vital factor in the treatment of stone because a good de of concern has been expressed in the use of silicon based preserv atives on stonework. Those responsible for the care and preservatio of medieval ecclesiatical buildings must achieve the right depth c penetration before gelling begins. A depth of 2 in (50 mm) should b obtained, and if not, the stone is at risk. The specialist must de with this situation as it requires great skill and experience.

If it is difficult to apply the full treatment when it is required, ther is a procedure that can be used as an interim measure. First, ascertai that no faulty rainwater channels (Fig. 5.10) exist, that no pointin has decayed, and that no other defects are making the stonewor wetter. If such defects exist, they must to be dealt with before an other treatment is commenced. Second, either remove the affecte stonework to a dry, safe place and consider replacing it with a cas copy, or provide a shelter for the area until the work can be don properly. If, as a last resource in this temporary situation it is cor sidered necessary to use a stone preservative, make absolutely certai that its use is supported by a recognised group or society that has n vested interest and is experienced in the work of preservation.

The recommended treatment is, first, to remove all dirt lightl with a hand spray and soft brush. Apply a hot lime poultice which i freshly slaked and approximately 20 mm thick, spread it evenly ove the entire profile, and cover the poultice with hessian and polythene The poultice should remain in this position for about three week and must be kept damp at all times; the poultice must be carefully re moved at the end of this period. This process will result in some di being removed with the lime, and the remainder will be soft enoug

**Fig. 5.10** Faulty rainwater channels

o remove by a brush with short bristles. The poultice is helpful for )ther reasons: it softens the calcium carbonate which tends to hold )n to the soot causing the natural salts to migrate; and it also makes he hard skin more receptive to the absorption of lime water, which s a further stage of the treatment. Numerous applications of lime vater are sprayed on to the surface to strengthen the weak areas. Finally, a protective coat which consists of lime putty, some pozzo- anic material, fine stone dust and a small quantity of casein is worked nto the surface to reduce the weathered texture and to take the effects of weathering. The result of this application fills the cavities vhich are caused by weathering, removes the salts and previous vashing, discourages the accumulation of dirt and prevents the sur- ace cavities from retaining moisture for any length of time. It has an additional benefit as it helps to replace deposits of calcium in the veakened stone which had been detrimentally affected when the oluble salts were removed. This process can only be undertaken by hose who have the expertise, but when properly administered this nethod extends the life of the original stone.

Stone is the material used in the building of walls, and the mason has the particular traditional skill required to build them. Masonry means the walling of blocks of natural stone quarried out of the ground. When considering walls in terms of 'caring' and 'preservation' we must understand and appreciate their structure, and an essential part of their stability is to ensure that the right kind of mortar is used. The mortar of medieval builders was a mixture of lime and sand, and as they frequently used the materials that were found in the vicinity, the mortar was variable in its consistency, with much of it deteriorating into dusty sand. Sometimes the medieval builders laid lead sheets between the joints, but this is not considered to be good practice as it breaks the continuity of the masonry and causes the edges of the stones to break away, reducing their bearing capacity quite considerably.

Reference has already been made to the thickness of medieval walls and there is no doubt that this is a major reason for their survival. We know of their success because they have withstood the test of time, but there were failures which were often due to the core and facing. In the early period most of the cores were formed of rubble constituting stones of various sizes and shapes, and these cavities were often inadequately filled (Fig. 3.8). When a weight was superimposed, the core, being relatively loose, found a different level to the facing stones and dislocated the structure. As this would occur at the initial stage of setting, the cores were subsequently improved in quality.

The basic principle of this part of the structure is to keep the combined thickness of all the bed-joints constant throughout core and facing in a given height of wall. The principle is to prevent unequal compression, and to achieve this the core must be packed with stone or brick so that only the minimum of void remains to be filled with mortar. Mortar, it must be remembered, shrinks while it is setting. To be successful in this process all cores should be level at frequent intervals of height. In a general sense, wide masonry joints usually have a longer life than fine joints because wide joints are able to take up the irregularities of bedding. The core and facing stones must be well bonded. In the walls there will be movement which need not necessarily be due to any weakness in the foundations. It is possible for an arch to exert certain pressures on a wall for years, and such an activity must have some consequence as it is an uneven load and has an effect on the structure. At this point reference can be made to the rule of the 'middle third', which states that if the main weight of a structure – described as a single force acting vertically through its centre of gravity – brings the load beyond the middle third of its base, then this results in a potential state of tension on its unloaded edge. If the total loading of a building is in good equilibrium, then its parts have mutual support, which implies that great consideration must be given to this aspect before administering any treatment

Panic serves no purpose in this situation; what is really required is a simple bonding into sound existing walls, or the transfer of a load into safe limits.

We return to a question asked in a earlier chapter: 'If it is considered that movement is taking place in a wall, is it right to stop it?' We have said that such movement can be localised at certain points and is harmless; it can, in fact, be regarded as an expansion joint – that is to say, it can be healthy as it is built into modern structures. If, on the other hand, it is thought that such a movement must be arrested, then it is necessary to determine where the remedy can best be applied It may be found that rebonding to sound existing work is satisfactory, having eradicated the reason for the movement. In other cases it may be essential to introduce supports or stays as the remedy. Walls have been strengthened in medieval buildings incorporating new architectural features; but it is possible in the thickness of the walls, to build stays which are both inconspicuous and very successful (Fig. 5.11).

When a building has to be re-roofed it is possible to combine a structural reinforcement with new work. A reinforced concrete slab can be tied into an existing wall provided that suitable gaps are left inside the parapets to allow for any movement in the concrete while it is setting. Tie-bars can be used in direct tension, and if spread adequately they can be very strong at their junctions with weaker materials. The ties that can be used are linked at each end with the reinforcement bars of reinforced concrete beams in the walls, which means that it is not necessary to have plates that are visible (Fig. 5.12).

The structure of the wall contains window sills and mullions, which are vulnerable and are liable to fracture; they also seem to rise

**Fig. 5.11** Inconspicuous stays in wall

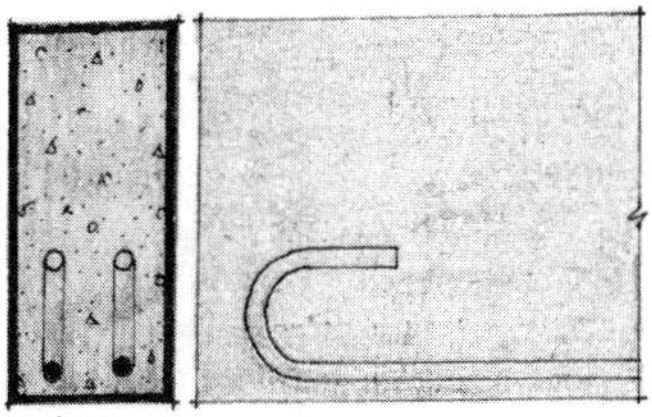


**Fig. 5.12** Reinforcement bars

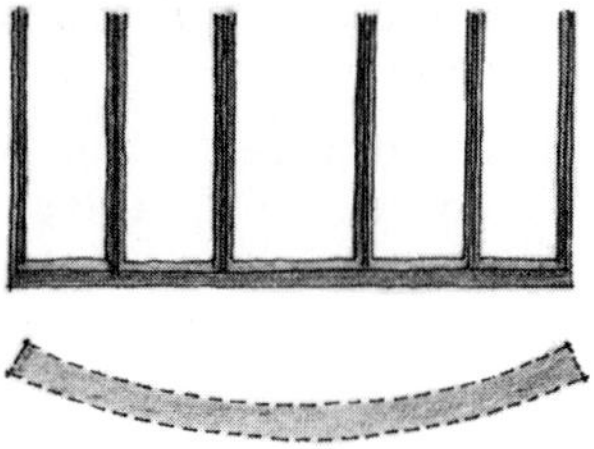

**Fig. 5.13** Sill under mullion

**Fig. 5.14** New work joined to old

when the walls around them sink. Medieval builders did not usually joint a sill immediately under a mullion because the smallest movement in the sill could split the mullion (Fig. 5.13). In dealing with this problem in wide windows it is possible to insert an inverted discharging arch which forces the wall below the sill to settle equally on each side. This kind of arch can be built into the wall and need not show externally.

At the beginning of this chapter it was stated that first-aid repairs are not satisfactory. This cannot be stressed too often and yet it is frequently happening in spite of all the warnings. Patched-up masonry is just not good enough. Each structure is different and reacts in various ways to weather and atmospheric conditions so that, in some cases, only parts of the wall may be affected and, in others, the whole of one side may be weather-beaten. It is true that patchy repairs can be disguised by cleaning the whole area by the use of a cheap substitute, such as a 'plastic' stone which is fixed to the original stone by hacking away the surface. This, however, is an outrageous method as it destroys the stone that it sets out to preserve; it is disastrous in its aesthetic consequences and will never achieve the mellow patina that appears on the surface of old stonework, even after cleaning.

To bring this chapter to a close it is important to consider the bonding of new material with existing material, and be aware it is possible to have a problem of settlement. Under weight the new joints will compress, which will be in automatic contention with the existing work that has long since found its level. It is almost impossible to avoid this kind of movement because new mortar will continue to compress until it has reached its final set, which can take as long as three or four months. The medieval builders were probably unaware of this danger as they built in vertical sections, going up to the eaves, in contrast to the present methods of taking up the structural walls course by course throughout. The problem of joining new work to old was overcome by medieval builders by rebating the upper faces of old toothing stones, which formed extra wide compressible bed joints where the new and old work joined (Fig. 5.14).

It may be wise to erect the new work in cement mortar for a width of three feet from the junction with the old to take full advantage of the rapid setting properties of cement.

# *Chapter 6*
# Arches, vaults, columns and piers

Arches and vaults are natural extensions of foundations, walls, columns and piers. The pointed arches (see Fig. 1.18) of the medieval period were vertically jointed at the apex because settlement would inevitably disturb the alignment of a pointed, moulded key-block. There are exceptions, such as external hood moulds (Fig. 6.1), where the joints at the lower part of the ribs (see Fig. 1.17) are grouped, above the springing, with the horizontal bed joints up to the point where the ribs separate. The ribs themselves are arranged so that they become an extension of the wall, behind which there are also horizontal bed joints.

In a sense it is remarkable that the principles that determine lines of thrust were so well understood in this period. Also, the fact that more weight was added vertically above the haunch of the arch contributed to the concept and development of Gothic design. It is important to remember that this principle can be applied when carrying out maintenance or restoration work. The lower parts of this construction were corbelled (Fig. 1.9). By diminishing the span the thrust became less and, as this developed, the gain of horizontal joints was recognised by extending the same principle to single arches. Horizontal joints of this type meet the arch mouldings at increasingly acute angles, and if problems involving this part of the structure are to be remedied, it is necessary to understand and appreciate their construction in greater detail than that given in Chapter 2.

There has been a tendency to regard the pointed arch as the distinctive feature of the Gothic period, but in fact it had been used by the Egyptians, Assyrians, pre-Hellenic Greeks and Etruscans a thousand years before the Christian era! The method of construction used by these early church builders, although mostly derived from Roman

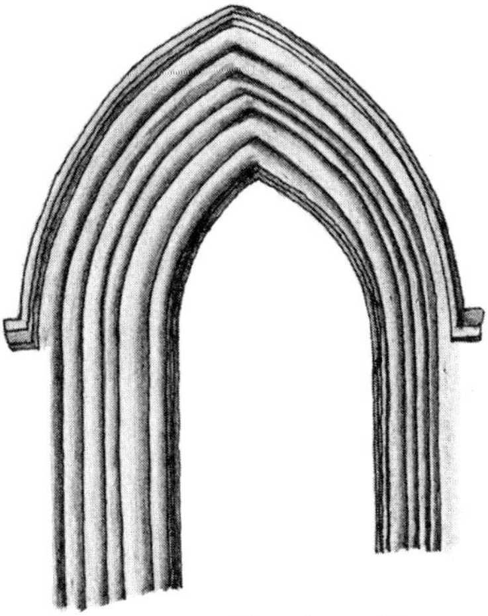

**Fig. 6.1** External hood mould

**Fig. 6.2** Pointed arch

architecture, had its own distinctive features. The builders of Roman arches used large voussoirs which, in the majority of cases, extended to the full thickness of the walls. The soffit was flush or was relieved by moulded panels which would be sunk (Fig. 6.2).

Early church builders used smaller stones which, in most cases, did not bend more than a few millimetres into the wall, with the space between being filled by rubble. Initially this was satisfactory as the wall above was either built of rubble throughout or was faced with ashlar that had a rubble core, but eventually this was not favoured and was replaced by a series of voussoirs on different planes. The first ring of voussoirs formed the central part of the soffit and was seldom more than half the width of the wall above. This carried the core of the wall and the outer rings which resulted in a partial projection each side until the outer rings were placed at a distance equal to the total thickness of the wall. An important advantage of this method was that it economised on the amount of centring required because the first ring became the centre as well as a support for the rings above. The 'springer' or bottom stone of each arch – except in very large ecclesiastical buildings – was one piece of stone which extended from front to back and side to side with, perhaps, two or more rings worked on it. This, of course, offered a solid bed from which the smaller stones of the different rings could

**Fig. 6.3** Cathedral arcade

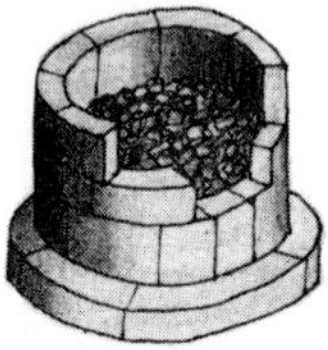

**Fig. 6.4** Columns: appearance of strength but innate weakness

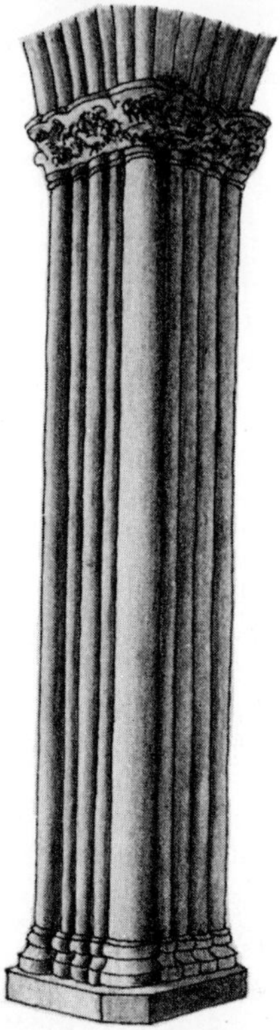

**Fig. 6.5** Clustered pier

spring, and at the same time it reduced the span and thrust of the arch. It was possible to use a large stone at this point as it was easy to hoist into position. In most cathedrals the arches of the arcades are built in three or four rings (Fig. 6.3).

A considerable amount of re-thinking occurred when the method of arch construction changed to meet the requirements of columns and piers. In England, as we have already mentioned, the columns, which were faced with ashlar, had rubble cores with the result that their very substantial girth gave the appearance of strength but had an innate weakness (Fig. 6.4). They were not a satisfactory seat for the various arches and ribs they had to support. A better solution was found in the rectangular pier; the cruciform was a further improvement; but the most satisfactory of all was the clustered pier (Fig. 6.5).

The early piers were rectangular and without moulds, but when arches started to appear a rib or pilaster was added to the back of each pier with a corresponding pilaster projecting from the wall on the other side of the aisle (Fig. 6.6). The pier became T-shaped then cruciform on plan, which meant that the arches thrown across the

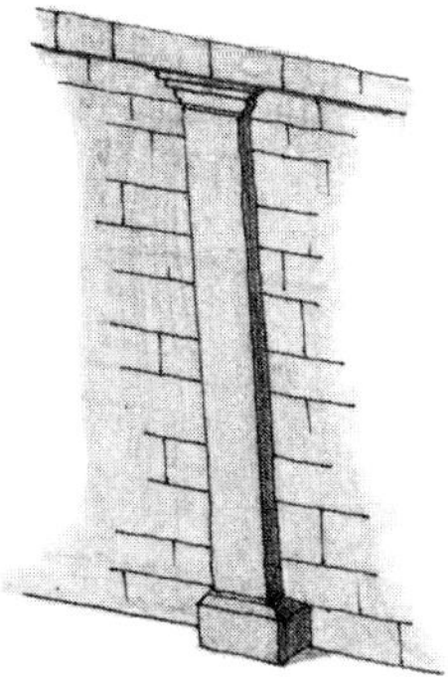

Fig. 6.6 Pilaster

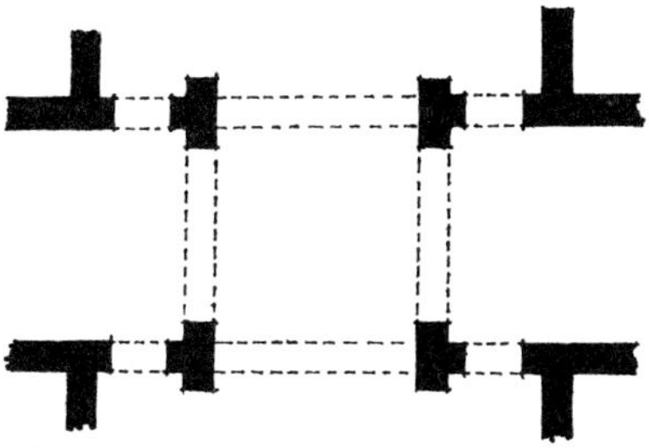

**Fig. 6.7** T-shaped pier

nave and the aisles had a substantial base from which to spring (Figs 6.6 and 6.7). A shaft was attached to the aisle side of the pier to support the side vaulting. Another shaft, on the nave side, was carried up to the underside of the vaulting ribs. The pier continued to be satisfactory until the introduction of the diagonal rib, which was not easy in the angle between the joinery ribs. It would have been difficult to bring so many points together if it were not for the creation of the clustered pier. Such was the design that each ring of an arch and each diagonal rib had its corresponding member in the pier below. This resulted in shafts being added to the pier or column which corresponded to the rings and vaulting ribs of the aisle and nave. This gave the appearance of a group of columns with each column supporting its own ring or rib. This is the clustered pier which, with other components, was part of the development of the Gothic style.

The vault, as in the case of the pointed arch, is not the prerogative of the Gothic period. The barrel vault (Fig. 1.12) and the intersecting vault (Fig. 6.8) were extensively used by the Egyptians, Assyrians and Romans.

Some early barrel vaults are very similar to those of the Romans. They are solid with the outer covering bedded on top of the vault itself. They often give the impression of being thick, but in fact are little more than 12 in. (305 mm) in most cases; this is particularly so with the intersecting vault, on which a protecting timber roof is superimposed. In a structural sense, the barrel vault is a disadvantage where there is an aisle since, as it is a continuous structure, it distributes its load equally over solids and voids, and similarly in the case of piers and arches. The intersecting vault has certain advantages over the barrel vault in that it focuses the thrust and weight of the vault at the points where they will be best received – that is, the piers. It also allows clerestory windows at the sides which can rise to the apex of the vault. Like so much medieval building the construction of the

**Fig. 6.8** Intersecting vault

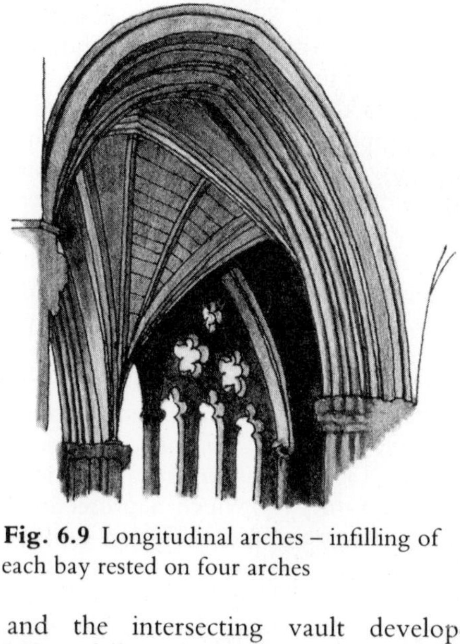

**Fig. 6.9** Longitudinal arches – infilling of each bay rested on four arches

barrel vault and the intersecting vault developed simultaneously. Modification followed and this was achieved by dividing the vault into square bays by transverse arches which sprang from pilasters (or attached columns) projecting from the wall or pier, and because their span was less than that of the vault, they gave the appearance of being below it. Simultaneously, arches were introduced

**Fig. 6.10** Diagonal ribs at groin lines

**Fig. 6.11** Square vault with semi-elliptical groins

ıd the infilling of each bay rested on four arches which focused ıe weight in a more efficient way on the piers (Fig. 6.9).

Not content with this development, the medieval builders took a ig step and introduced diagonal ribs at the lines of intersection groin lines) of the vault (Fig. 6.10). This became a ribbed vault – disnguishing it from a groined or intersecting vault – and its construcon was composed of a structural framework of transverse arches, ngitudinal arches, diagonal ribs and the web (infilling) which rested ı the frame. The web, which only had its own weight to carry, ›uld be quite thin and in a sense was quite independent of the walls. ll this meant that a certain principle had been reached which comned the thrusts at given points, thus paving the way for the later velopments of Gothic architecture.

In assessing any necessary work, careful observation has to be ade because, first, the ribs will not always appear to be built indendently of the web (Fig. 2.16) (or infilling) and, second, the web is ›t lighter than in an ordinary groined vault. It can be deduced from is that although the rib may have given strength to the weakest line the vault, its primary purpose was to give a pleasing aesthetic fect. There was controversy over the use of diagonal ribs, but that beyond the scope of this book. The important thing is that, with e introduction of the rib, there followed the solution to the probn of covering large spans with stone. As may be expected, certain fficulties were encountered that had not previously been conlered. In the case of a square vault which has no ribs and where the hes are semi-circular, the groins are semi-elliptical with a weakss in form (Fig. 6.11). The early builders attempted to make the ›s segmental or elliptical, or semi-circular. Many of the early vaults re over aisles, which usually involved a small span where the build- could 'manoeuvre' their materials to fit the requirements. When gonal ribs are added the entire structure is altered: the ribs have to ry the weight of the infilling and must therefore be very strong.

Let us take two typical situations and use them to illustrate the fact t it is possible to achieve satisfactory results with a minimal effort

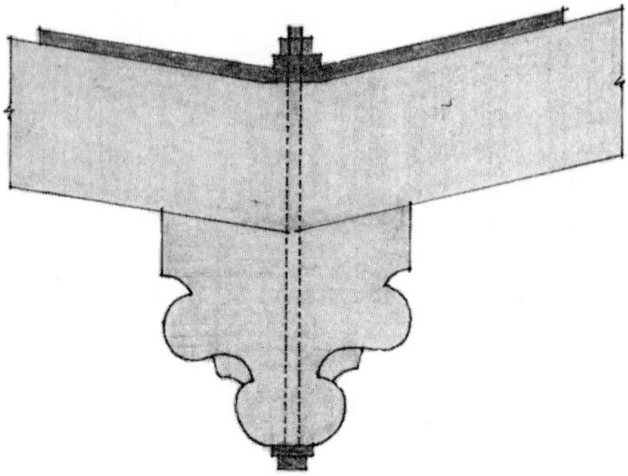

**Fig. 6.12** Rib failure

in caring and preserving the fabric. A vault, having a 'boss' whic weighs half a ton, has dropped, is cracked and is splitting awa from each of the ribs which support it. The ribs have also bee affected and their backs have crushed causing them to bulge belo their lines of curvature. At first sight this can be rather forbiddin but is not a major problem. In the first place the ribs have to b strengthened, and to do this holes will be drilled through the from the fillet to the upper surface of the vault. Gun-metal stri will be fitted to the fillet and will be bolted up with gun-met bolts through holes on the upper surface of the vault. Wi great care these bolts will then be tightened with the result that t ribs will be brought into correct alignment. Being at such a heig the metal strip(s) will follow very faithfully the lines of the fro fillet(s) and will hardly be visible from ground level (Fig. 6.12).

As another example, let us take a building, of the Perpendicul phase in which the transepts are dated later than the nave. When t transepts were added transverse arches were built to divide the ea end of the nave aisles from the new transepts. Instead of rebuildi and enlarging the piers of the nave arcades which were to take t weight and thrust of the new arches, the medieval builders insert corbels (Fig. 1.9) which were used as springing for the transver arches. The slender piers were unable to cope with the cross-thrus and, by degrees, bent outwards into the nave. At a much later da when the problem was becoming alarming, iron tie-rods were plac across each transverse arch at springing level; they passed throu the centre of each corbel, and ended up in the nave with a plate – most unpleasant sight from an aesthetic point of view. It function for a time, but in due course the ends of the tie-rods rusted and sp the corbels – the components that were supposed to be carrying t weight of the arches. It was decided that the affected arches wou need to be shored up, that steel joists should be embedded in co crete the thickness of the cross-walls immediately above the tra verse arches, and that heels should be incorporated to grip each e

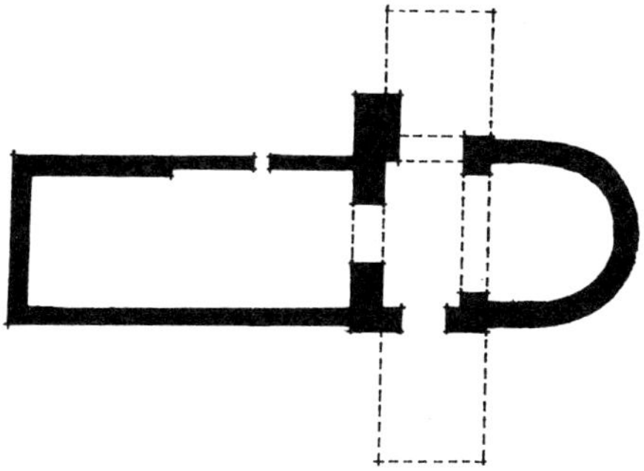

**Fig. 6.13** Transept added

ɔ that the thrusts of the arches below could be held. After this the ·on rods were removed from the corbels with difficulty, and the vhole section was restored to its original condition and made struc-ırally sound (Fig. 6.13).

In Chapter 5 we considered, among other things, stonework and valls. In this chapter attention has been given to the supports and ıperstructure and it is therefore, appropriate to include the ways ıd means of dealing with the care and preservation of the fabric om a practical point of view; that is, the use of scaffolding and ıoring. We shall deal with them in that order.

Scaffolding, including ladders, guard rails and platforms, on which considerable amount of work occurs, is used to provide a tempor-y structure in order to gain access to a building that is beyond ɔrmal reach from the ground. It is convenient to describe two ·rms of scaffold: 'independent' scaffold (Fig. 6.14) and 'putlog' scaf-ld (Fig. 6.15). These will be made of tubular steel, or tubular alu-inium alloy or timber. The independent scaffold has two rows of andards tied together by cross-members with transoms. One of the lvantages of this form of scaffold is that it needs no support from e building and can be used with framed structures. Nevertheless, ·ery scaffold is required to be secured to the building and this can : done by the use of the horizontal tube, called a bridle, which bears ı the inside of the wall – preferably through a window opening – .d is connected to the main frame by cross-members. If no suitable ɔening is available, the scaffold will require the addition of struts ɔm the ground as raking tubes, which must be inclined towards the ıilding (Fig. 6.16).

The 'putlog' scaffold is a single row of uprights which are set at a fficient distance from the wall to give adequate space for a working ıtform. The uprights are joined by horizontal ledgers which are d to the building by cross-pieces, giving this method of scaffold-ȝ its name. Again it must be stressed that the erection of scaffold-ȝ should not be contemplated by anyone other than those who are mpetent and experienced in this field, not only because of health

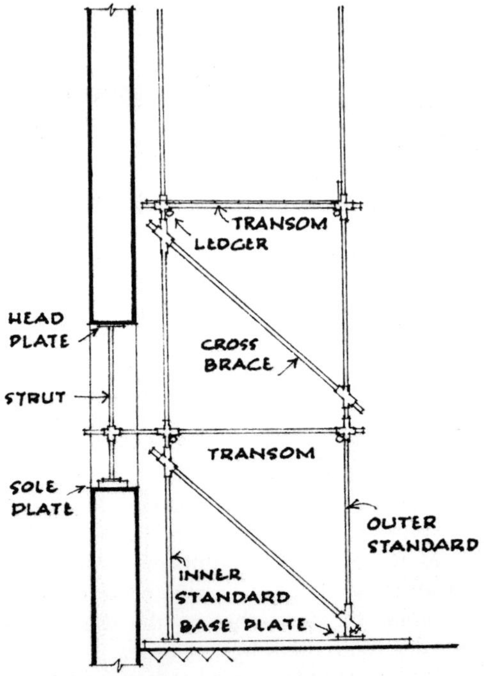


**Fig. 6.14** Independent scaffold

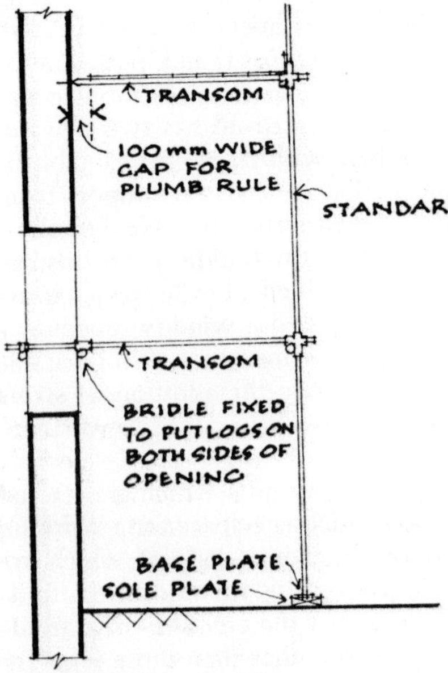


**Fig. 6.15** Putlog scaffold

**Fig. 6.16** Struts

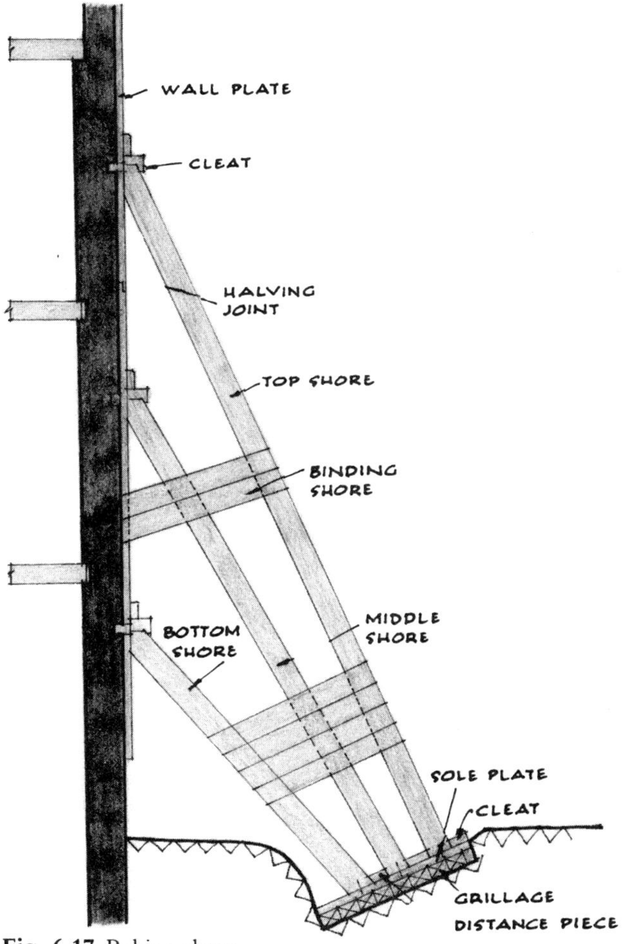


**Fig. 6.17** Raking shore

and safety which, of course, are vital, but because there are statutory requirements in the composition of a scaffold. We shall not discuss those items here because they are many and varied and, in any case will be known to the contractor.

Although, theoretically, shoring is considered to be a temporary support to a building as required by regulations, buildings have been seen to be propped up in this way for long and indefinite periods! As in scaffolding, there are three basic systems of shoring – the raking shore (Fig. 6.17), the dead shore (Fig. 6.18), and the flying shore (Fig. 6.19) – each of which has its own function, although combinations of all three will occasionally be required.

The principle of the raking shore is to transfer the floor and wall loads to the ground by sloping rakers. With this method it is essen-

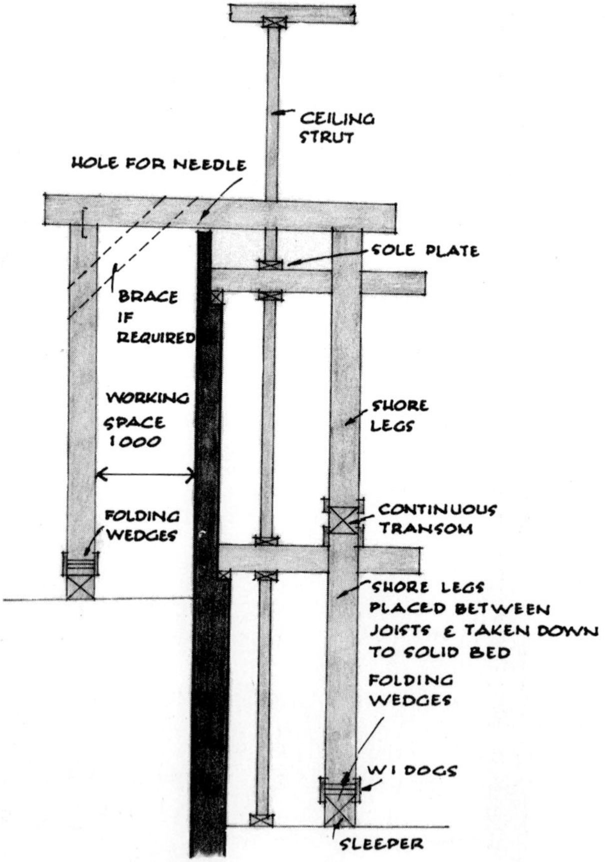


**Fig. 6.18** Dead shore

tial that the rakers are set in the correct position to take maximum load. The centreline of the rakers should intersect with the centrelines of the wall or floor bearing. A dead shore is used to support dead loads which have a vertical-downwards action. Basically it is a vertical prop or shore with a head plate, sole plate and a means of easing and tightening the shore. One method used frequently employs two shore legs which are connected over their heads by a horizontal beam transferring the load to the shore legs and on to the bearing surface, which must be solid. The flying shore has a similar function to the raking shore, but with the added advantage of giving a clear working area beneath the shoring. This type of shore can be used on parallel walls, provided the area between them is not excessive. As in the case of scaffolding, the use of shoring is strictly under the discipline of the works department and the architect in charge, who will advise and be responsible for such a structure.

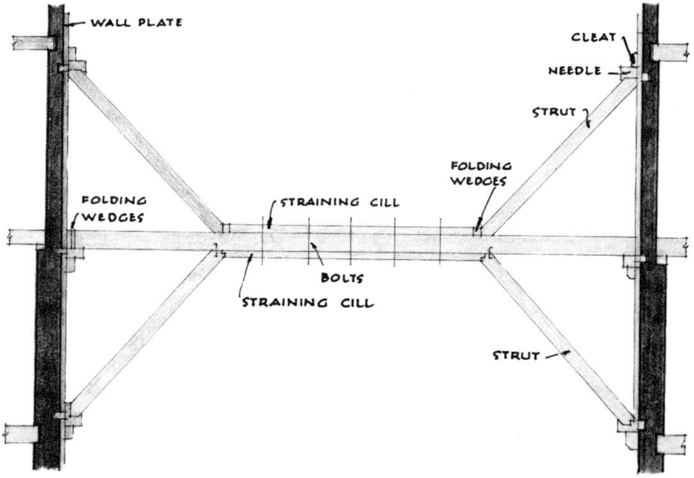


**Fig. 6.19** Single flying shore

Particular care will be needed in the use of shoring or scaffolding in order to prevent any kind of damage to medieval buildings. It was rather fortuitous that the builders of the medieval period very often omitted to fill up the original 'putlogs', and where they are available they can be used. It will be wise to make certain that they have not been mutilated or weakened by the weather and/or birds who, over the centuries, have gained access to the core. When shoring or scaffolding is used and medieval walls are pierced in order to insert a bearing (or needle), care must be taken as the core will pour out of the hole in the form of dust. Shoring problems in particular are usually individual and require all the expertise that is available; this also applies to scaffolding. So too should all available expertise and knowledge be used in the care and preservation of these architectural treasures.

# *Chapter 7*
# Woodwork

The medieval carpenters were experts in the use of simple tools, obtaining remarkably fine surfaces by splitting boards and panels with wedges and using an adze (Fig. 7.1) to make heavy timbers smooth. There have been many attempts to imitate them, but not with a great deal of success and in any case this is not justified because the original methods are remote from the techniques in use today, mainly due to the fact that in those early days so much that was accomplished was spontaneous and individual.

A cursory glance, quite apart from a detailed investigation, soon indicates the constrast between present-day methods and the medieval achievements. There appears to be no economy in the timberwork of the medieval craftsman, and several features underline this. In the first place, there was a surplus of wood in excess of that required to carry the loads. This provided ample resources of strength, giving built-in life to the structure which, in any other circumstances, would have failed due to age. Many cathedrals and churches would

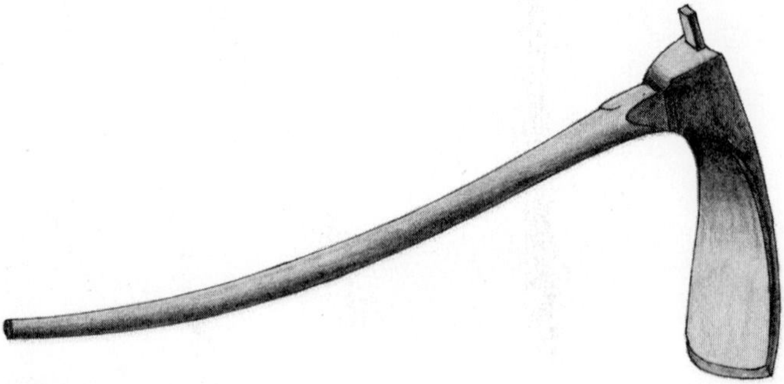

**Fig. 7.1** Adze

**Fig. 7.2** Medieval purlins

**Fig. 7.3** Purlins with greater depth at right angles to plane

have disappeared years ago if the builders had limited the initial strength to this part of the structure. The second feature is the medieval practice of laying rafters and purlins flat (Fig. 7.2) instead of placing the greater depth of each timber at right angles to the plane of the roof, as has been the practice for many years (Fig. 7.3) The medieval system gave the impression of strength, but the timbers were not being used to their best structural advantage. The third feature was the size of the timbers used, which were large in length and girth and proved to be a distinct advantage in counteracting the

**Fig. 7.4** Pitched roofs

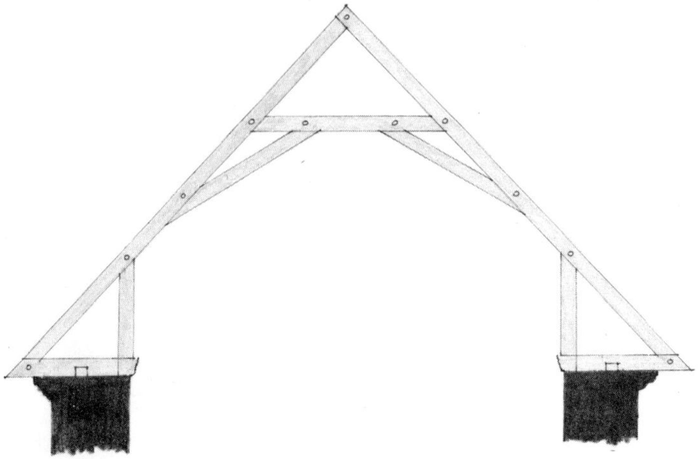

**Fig. 7.5** Heads of rafters (Gothic)

possibility of decay. If any decay occurs it will occur near the joints, and fewer joints will reduce the risk of decay.

Another interesting aspect of medieval woodwork, in comparison to present-day techniques, is the construction of pitched roofs (Fig. 7.4). It is rare in present building construction to omit the ridge-piece running along the ridge of the roof which ensures that the heads of the rafters are in correct alignment (Fig. 7.5). In the medieval period this part of the roof structure was missing, and each pair of rafters was secured with a 'halved and pinned' joint (Fig. 7.6). The carpenters of this generation made use of the tapered oak peg or pin, which was fixed leaving its head slightly projecting (Fig. 7.7.) When the woodwork shrank the peg could be inserted further to ensure more security in the joint. This method had limitations because timber is constantly active and it is difficult to keep joints tight; they are also liable, of course, to be attacked by the wood-boring beetles. This system of medieval construction presents certain problems today, but there are methods of dealing with it. Such a situation arose with nave trusses that were built towards the end of the fifteenth century, and in this case iron straps were used at important joints

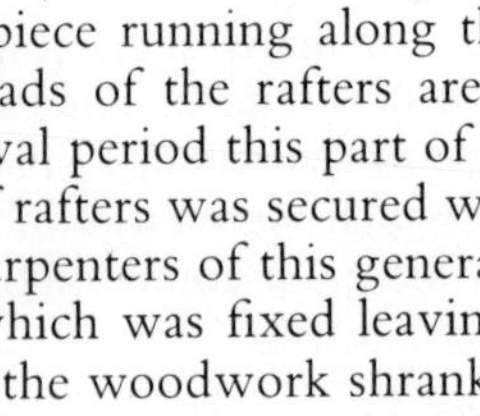

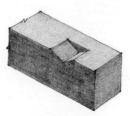

**Fig. 7.6** Halved joint

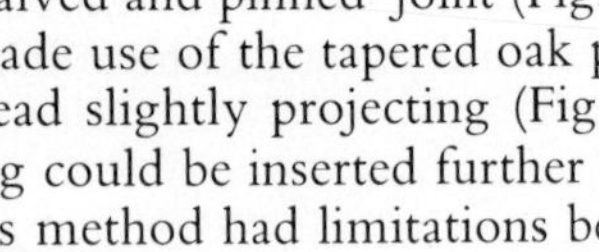

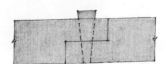

**Fig. 7.7** Oak peg

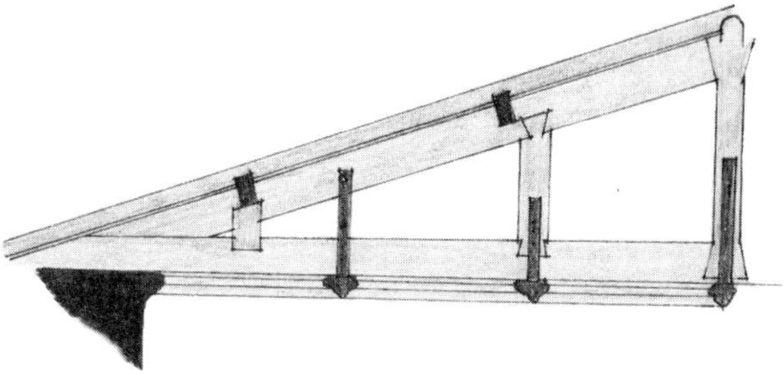

**Fig. 7.8** Straps

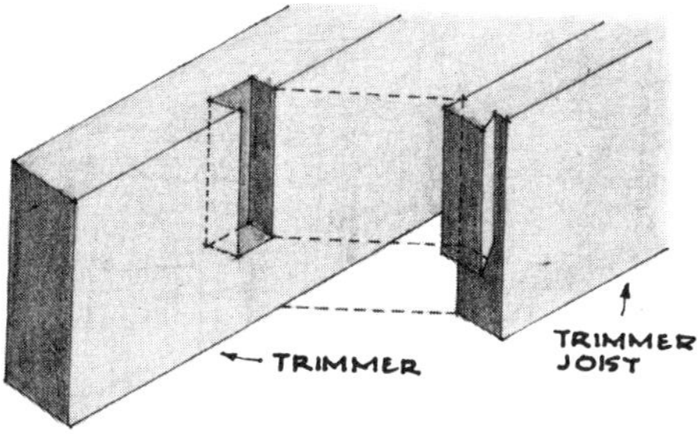


**Fig. 7.9** Dovetailed joints

(Fig. 7.8). The vertical members of the trusses ended in dovetailed joints, as shown in Fig. 7.9, which were designed to cope with the tension in a way that is quite divorced from modern methods. The ceiling, which was of a slightly later date, was suspended beneath the trusses by wooden straps pinned to both sides of each tie-beam (Fig. 7.10).

This chapter is mainly concerned with an appreciation and understanding of at least some of the destructive agents that can be quite devastating in older buildings. Wood can, of course, be inherently defective when it is first used in a building, but woodwork that has been in position for centuries is an academic proposition. When wood is used for repairs or in restoration, this is another matter and is very important. Destructive agents, such as wood-boring beetles or fungi which concentrate on the sapwood of new hardwood, can have infected the timbers and could still be active. Some of the commonest defects are natural splits in the timber, which are technically called 'shakes'. In most instances 'shakes' occur as the result of shrinkage during the process of seasoning or where there are inherent weaknesses; and this is when the wood is most vulnerable to attack. Shrinkage inevitably makes the wood structurally weak, and if the shrinkage is particularly severe it allows moisture to enter the heart of the timber. It also provides entry points for wood-boring beetles. At the risk of stating the obvious, it is stressed that thoroughly sea-

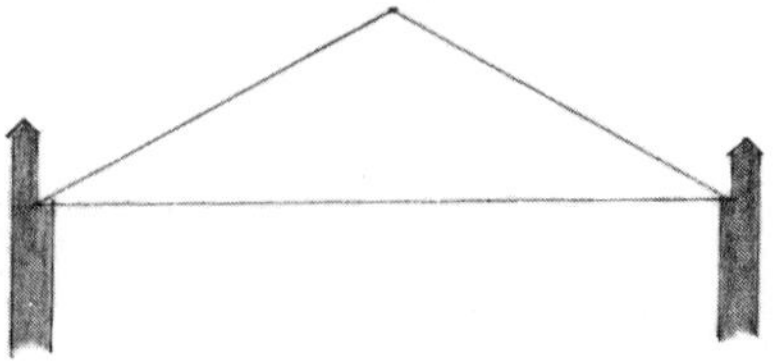

**Fig. 7.10** Tie-beam

**Fig. 7.11** Rubbish above vaults

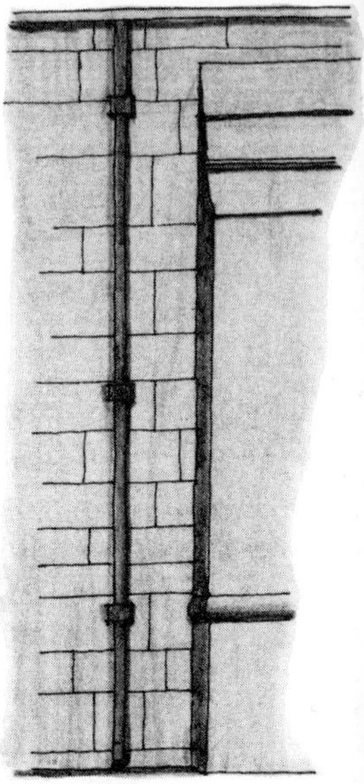

**Fig. 7.12** Gutter and downpipe

soned timber must be used for any repair work. Apart from any other reason, it is intended that the building will last for another few hundred years! To achieve this the conditions must be dry otherwise the soundest timber may decay. It is equally important and essential to have adequate ventilation. Although not as dangerous as other agents, accumulated dirt can be a source of danger to sound timber as it has a tendency to hold moisture. Many discoveries have been made when attending to structural problems in roof timbers: for example, rubbish has been used to fill the voids in the roof space above the vaults (Fig. 7.11); and wood chippings and sawdust have been found among rubbish. An investigation into death-watch beetle in a roof found that the pockets of the roof were alive with grubs and had been a breeding ground for a very long time.

Although old woodwork can be fundamentally sound, it may be affected by fungal attack. It can be treated with a preservative, but for this kind of treatment the timber must be dry. The treatment consists of a local injection of clear organic solvent-type preservative which can be applied by a type of plastic injector. This is in the form of a plug which is driven into a hole that has already been bored. The injector penetrates until it is flush with the surface. If it is found that the timber is not thick enough to take the full length of the plug, the plug should be trimmed to a suitable length before insertion. It is usual to drill a hole for the injector plug about ½ in (13 mm) above the affected area. The depth of hole should be related to the thickness of timber. For the injection of the preservative there is a standard grease gun connection and the time involved is about two to four minutes at a pressure of three newtons per square metre (3 N $m^{-2}$), which is considered adequate. After the treatment is completed the plug is driven into the hole, or the top of the plug is cut off and the small remaining hole is plugged with a suitable filler. Treated timber must not be painted until the solvents in the preservative have fully evaporated. There are certain precautions that must be observed in the whole process, and these will be under the direction of the specialist operator.

Dry rot is a misleading term in some respects, except that the infection does spread to dry timber, leaving it dead and brittle with a distinctive odour. It is necessary to understand the process of this destructive agent which causes so much damage to old buildings. Its life cycle starts with a spore which is very resilient to extreme temperatures and has a long lifespan. Several fungi cause the decay, and wood that is in a warm, damp and badly ventilated position is most vulnerable. The fungus develops rapidly and throws out microscopic hollow threads which spread over the surface of the wood forming a grey network covering which sometimes has blue-grey or yellow patches. If conditions are very bad the hyphae may be formed in the shape of cotton-wool masses which will be snow-white in colour with bright yellow patches. To summarise the process, the mycelium develops into a strong, fleshy substance known as a fruit body, which has a mushroom appearance and is dark red or brown with a white edge and a surface that resembles a sponge. It is pitted with holes and is corrugated; it is a sinister object with an attractive appearance. Numerous spores are produced on the surface and can easily be transmitted by vermin, insects and air currents. Drops of moisture form on the fungus and hang there – a process known as weeping!

A further destructive activity of the fungus is its ability to produce strands which spread in all directions, penetrating mortar. These strands can also channel water from the damp original site of dry rot to dry wood, thereby extending the disease. In the development of the fungus the fibres of the woodwork are attracted by feeding on the cell walls which break down gradually, eventually reducing the woodwork to powder when pressurised by a finger touch – hence the name applied to the rot. Dry rot has a dull red-brown appearance; the weight of the timber is reduced and its strength is limited, eventually causing it to collapse.

In this chapter reference has been made to a treatment that can be applied either as a precaution or to prevent this kind of occurrence, which can have very serious consequences. The woodwork must be kept dry, and to achieve this the eaves, gutters, downpipes and roof coverings must be constantly inspected and maintained (Fig. 7.12). Failure to repair any defects will accelerate decay.

Joists and wall plates should be treated with a preservative, and if they are seriously affected should be removed and replaced without delay. Where structural timbers have been infected, but not weakened, by the fungus each piece of infected wood should be removed and, preferably, burnt with any other remains of the infected area, such as shavings, dirt and sawdust. If new woodwork is inserted it must be treated on each face to avoid any infection. It would be advisable to avoid introducing any new wood fixings into a wall. Other fungal decays can occur but they are not very serious and do not spread to sound timber.

Insect attack is another destructive agency in woodwork, but it is not usually as serious as fungal attack because the affected area is limited to the tunnel(s) within it. This is especially true in medieval buildings, largely due to the enormous sections of timber used. Even half infection will not reduce the strength of these members, but that is not to suggest that they can be given any less serious attention. In most cases all that is required is a strengthening of the existing woodwork. The death-watch beetle, the biggest culprit of all, attacks well-matured wood. The beetles lay their eggs in holes and cracks in the wood, and the grubs (white larvae), which hatch out of eggs, are about ¼ in. (6 mm) long. After boring into the wood for about eighteen months or more they develop into chrysalises, about August, near the surface of the wood. The winged beetle forms in a few weeks after pupation and does not break surface until the following spring. Most damage is done during the larvae stage when the grubs bore numerous tunnels, which measure about ⅛ in. (3 mm) in diameter, within the timber and produce a quantity of dust during the whole process. In advanced cases most of the interior of the affected wood members are reduced to powder. The conditions of poor ventilation and dampness associated with dry rot are similarly conducive to beetle attack, which suggests that any treatment of infested structural woodwork includes the provision of adequate general ventilation and air space around built-in ends of members. Badly infected wood will have to be removed and replaced by sound timber which is free from sapwood.

A number of proprietary insecticides are available, but these will be administered by the experts. Prior to applying the solution liberally with a spray or brush, the timber should be thoroughly brushed and vacuumed to remove as much dust as possible. It is necessary to give several applications to make sure that the preservative has penetrated sufficiently. Creosote can be used if it is not considered offensive and if there is no objection to discoloration, but this treatment should be repeated every three or four years. Two other species of insect that attack furniture, joinery and panelling are the common furniture beetle and the powder post beetle.

Several proprietary solutions are available for treating infested timber; they are applied to the surface by brush during the spring and

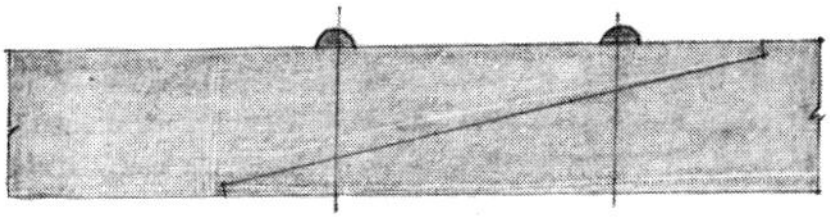

**Fig. 7.13** Scarfing

summer. To be most effective several applications are necessary.

We note, in passing, the usefulness of bats – not just in the belfry but in the roof. They play an important role and can be most efficient scavengers. The author has spent many hours in the roof of an English cathedral and, in the gloom of the massive roof structures, has been aware of the aerial activity of these creatures. There are very good reasons for not destroying them and they make a useful contribution to the life of roof woodwork. To determine when old timber should be replaced by new is a matter of professional judgement following a careful examination of suspected areas. These areas, whether they have been attacked by fungi or beetle, should be attended to at once. It is not difficult to join new work to an existing structure; it is known as 'scarfing ' (Fig. 7.13).

Where wood is built into walls it may be necessary to spread the work over as wide an area as possible to make certain that all infection is removed. The architect will provide a specification for both fungal and pest-eradication, and this should be adhered to at all times.

# *Chapter 8*
# Floors, windows and roofs

There is an inherent danger in thinking that, when the major structural problems in the care and preservation of cathedrals and churches have been attended to, the other parts of the work are not as important. This is a grave error of judgement, as the fabric is made up of many parts each of which is essential and integral to the whole. If we now turn our attention to these parts we may realise their importance to the remainder of the structure.

## Floors

The neglect of floors can cause a great deal of deterioration to the fabric and involve enormous expense as this is where damp can enter a building and leave a trail of wreckage in the form of dry rot. This was considered more fully in Chapter 5.

When attending to floors care must be taken to ensure that the maintenance or restoration is not so economic and austere that it spoils the aesthetic beauty of the original work. On the other hand, extravagant attention can detract from and destroy the authenticity of medieval craftsmanship. Brass grave slabs (Fig. 8.1) and medieval encaustic tiles must be treated with the greatest respect.

As slabs and tiles were designed to be laid on a horizontal plane they must remain this way; and the graves which have their memorials over them should not be removed. A balanced judgement should be exercised in deciding how to attend to uneven paving in aisles and walking areas, as it is necessary to retain the irregular charm while guarding against the destructive effects of wear. This requires sensitive treatment, because overexposing the paving to considerable pedestrian traffic will cause a rapid obliteration of

**Fig. 8.1** Brass grave slab

pattern work. When it is absolutely necessary to do work on these floors – such as re-laying the stones and tiles – great care must be taken. Under certain conditions it can be an advantage to treat the beds of the paving slabs with an impervious material before they are re-laid.

It is important to remember that during the nineteenth century the level of some of these floors may have been altered as there was a tendency to level the naves and transepts and increase the number of steps in the chancel up to the altar (Fig. 8.2). Consideration must therefore be given to their levels and the position of the steps. Medieval floors usually followed the fall of the ground, and it is worthwhile retaining the natural slope. Extra care will be required

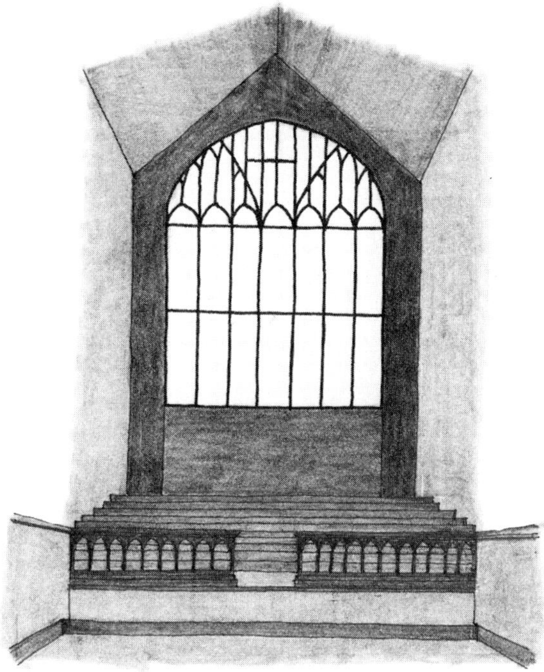

**Fig. 8.2** Steps in chancel

**Fig. 8.3** Sedilia

in certain other parts of the building; for example, in the sanctuary close attention will need to be given to the levels of the sedili (Fig. 8.3) and piscina (Fig. 3.1), which are normally in their origina positions, due to rearrangement of the choir since the introduction o various liturgies. If the floor requires extensive alteration it will b seen that the early floors in ecclesiastical buildings did not have th substantial bed that is put into modern buildings. As this bed i missing in most cases, it should be added.

## Windows

This aspect of cathedrals and churches is a most valuable part of ou heritage and will require a great deal of thought. In medieval times i was common practice to fix iron saddle-bars and upright stanchion across the window openings (Fig. 8.4). It is probable that they wer originally intended as anti-intruder devices as well as supports t weak lead glazing. They have been, and can still be, a serious sourc of trouble and a serious hazard to the glazing, and as they ca threaten the aesthetic and structural condition they must be we maintained.

In later Gothic buildings windows were an integral part in th progressive dissipation of rigidity from buttress and pier, through curtain wall to mullion (Fig. 8.5), transom (Fig. 8.6) and tracer (Fig. 2.35). Their importance is realised when we examine almos any Gothic building externally. Rustless steel alloys are very expens ive and are probably beyond the scope of most local financial re sources, but when set against the long-term policy they will be a investment. The dangers in the use of iron in stonework have bee discussed in Chapter 6, and any treatment must be most carefully con sidered. In the case of stanchions, the feet should be cut ½ in. (13 mm above the stone sill; and if saddle-bars are taken through mullion

**Fig. 8.4** Saddle-bars

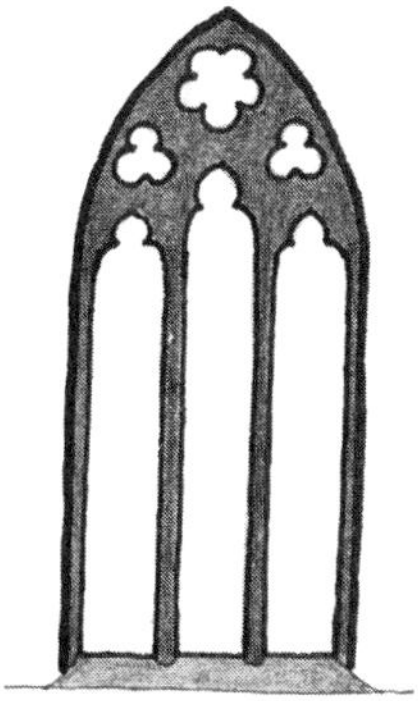

**Fig. 8.5** Mullion

**Fig. 8.6**
Transom

**Fig. 8.7** Saddle-bars
from one window
to another

they should not be continuous from one window opening to another (Fig. 8.7). If these fixtures are necessary they should be made of bronze, thus removing the need for painting, which is an important aspect when dealing with many of the windows of the Perpendicular

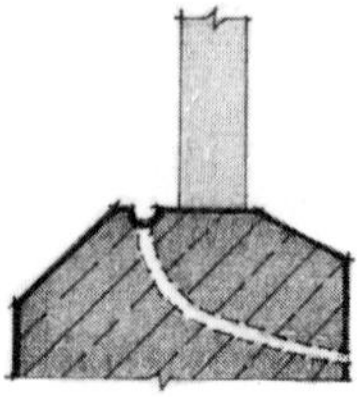

**Fig. 8.8.**
Stone sill outlet

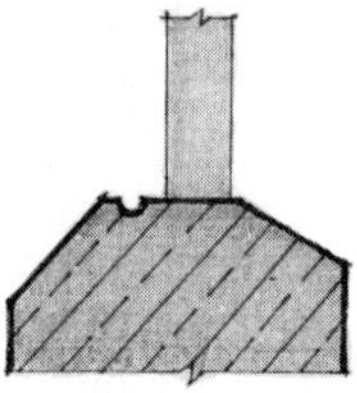

**Fig. 8.9**
Evaporator

phase as they can be almost inaccessible and are difficult to maintain on a regular basis. There is a justifiable complaint by the artists about the upright stanchions which leave little or no room to work on the glass. Saddle-bars, however, do not present the same difficulty. With the co-operation of the architect the artist can have the stanchions clear of the glass so that light enters behind them.

In medieval buildings the fixed lights of the windows can cause condensation which runs down the face of the window and causes considerable staining on the walls. This can be remedied by cutting a groove in the stone window sill, but unless there is an adequate outlet this can cause other problems (Fig. 8.8). An alternative method is to have a watertight gutter of copper channel projecting from the sill inside the glazing; this forms a reservoir and as there is a limited amount of water, it evaporates (Fig. 8.9).

It would seem that the windows of early cathedrals and churches were not considered for ventilation, which is more understandable in cathedrals than in churches because of the height involved. Where opening lights have been introduced they must be placed in suitable and inconspicuous positions. The glazing should be in the hands of a specialist who deals with preservation and restoration. He should be an experienced artist and craftsperson and is required to consider the causes, their spacing and design – especially in cusping (Fig. 8.10) and tracery (Fig. 2.26).

The art of making stained glass has changed very little over the centuries, and even today is carried out by hand. It is lengthy and complicated because it involves a lot of minute detail and a number of processes.

## Roofs

It would not be an overstatement to say that the roof is that part of the structure that requires most attention both in inspection and maintenance. We remind ourselves that the basic function of the roof is to deal adequately with the elements – mainly rain and, in some areas, snow – disposing of it at given points which, in themselves, are danger points and must have regular inspections as they can be

**Fig. 8.10** Cusping

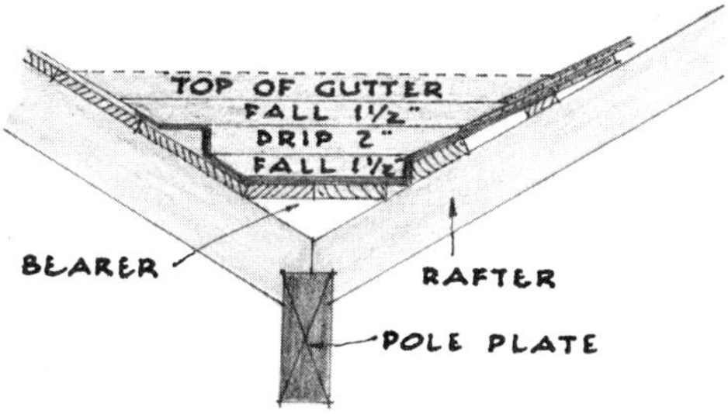


**Fig. 8.11** Internal valley

the source of extensive and endless trouble and expense. Inaccessible and unattended places can be neglected; for example, gutters, internal valleys (Fig. 8.11) and parts that abut against other structures. Certain symptoms become apparent: a slate roof which appears satisfactory at a cursory glance can, on closer examination, be seen to be laminating and will not function properly much longer; or lead can show lines of fatigue which will soon become fractures.

One of the first questions that must be asked is: 'Does the roof require repair or renewal?' In order that a decision can be reached, certain criteria have to be considered, for example: what is the remaining life of the material(s)?; is it necessary to renew it in its entirety?; is it an integral part of the architectural design?; which is the more economic in every sense? Most of the answers to these questions will be determined by the material used to cover the roof. If it is a lead roof and has cracks it can be repaired by 'burning'; if it is a copper roof, it is not possible to do a patch job. Tiled roofs can present problems – largely due to corrosion of the nails that fix the tiles to

**Fig. 8.12** Battens

the battens (Fig. 8.12) – as the tiles tend to fall with the leaves before winter.

There is no short cut in dealing with this situation; the entire roof will need to be stripped and all the tiles re-hung. This may be regarded as drastic and some church authorities may shudder at the thought and abandon the whole idea, but when it is realised that a few faulty tiles suggest that numerous others are barely holding, a different attitude may prevail and a proper decision may be reached. The roof will need to be completely stripped, and by doing this any failure of other fixtures will be seen, such as battens that may have perished. This situation can also arise where a roof has to be recovered with an entirely different material. Although it may be cheaper, it can change the appearance of the building entirely, and this will need to be considered with extreme care.

A roofing material that was used extensively on ecclesiastical buildings was lead. A great deal of concern has been expressed in recent years about the corrosion of this material. In one case deterio-

**Fig. 8.13** Lead support and framing

ration took place within ten years on a cathedral roof, and this was after it had been re-roofed! The symptons of lead corrosion show blistering of the external surface and corrosion of the lead sheet.

Lead has many virtues as a roof covering: it is easily dressed and can be adapted to many unusual and irregular shapes; it has considerable durability, but it must have a proper support and fixing (Fig. 8.13). One of its well-known disadvantages – mainly when it is improperly used – is that it 'creeps'; that is, thermal movements take place which accumulate, and it often fails to return to its original position. Sheet lead has been widely used and is regarded as the roof covering with the longest life. Leadwork, milled and cast, can be re-used as it can be melted down and re-cast. If sheet lead is used for roofing it must be continuously supported. When the boarding has been adequately prepared, building paper should be used as an underlay, which is essential because sheet lead must not be in contact with oak which may be attacked by tannic acid.

When sheets of lead are re-laid the choice has to be made between lapped junctions over a wooden roll and tightly dressed open roll or standing welts. Unless there is a lot of pedestrian traffic the open roll is the best method – especially if there is any kind of fall in the roof – because it is tight and provides a continuous grip, reducing the possibility of any slipping of the sheets of lead. It will be necessary to keep a careful watch for damage that can be done to lead work by the moisture that comes out of lichen, which contains acid.

The use of copper for roofing has been in practice for many years. This can be identified by the green 'patina' – an inherent activity of the material – which produces a most pleasing aesthetic feature. Also, copper is less dense than lead. There is, however, a danger in the use of copper: it is prone to fatigue and may eventually crack due

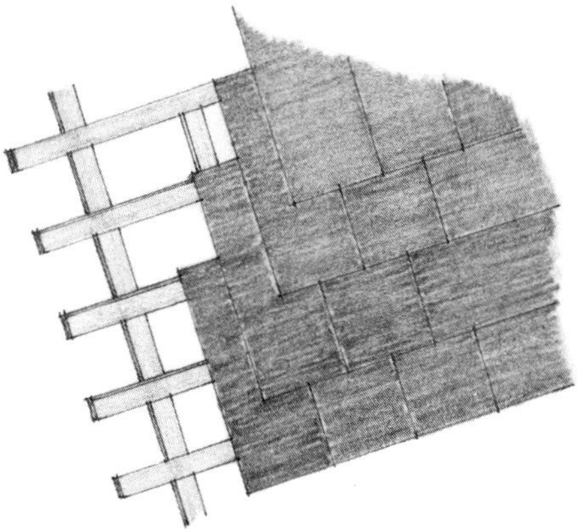

**Fig. 8.14** Slates: repaired diagonally

**Fig. 8.15** Tiles and battens

to handling when it was originally dressed or due to 'drumming' through lack of sufficient support. If a copper roof has shown faults it is better dealt with in its entirety rather than by first-aid repairs. By dealing with the entire roof there is an opportunity to examine other parts of the structure which may be at fault by, perhaps, not having the even continuous support that it requires. Felting will be required to avoid chafing, but this should be non-bituminous and should be fixed by copper nails with butt joints. Copper for re-roofing will be specified by the architect, who will also stipulate the size and laying method.

Other materials are available, but as yet have not had time to prove their suitability. One of these is aluminium which, in due course, will probably take its place beside copper and lead. Slates and tiles are the roofing materials used on a large number of ecclesiastical buildings. If an area of the roof is affected it can be cut out for repair, and it is better to work diagonally upwards from the eaves to avoid damage to other fixings (Fig. 8.14).

Tiles, which hang over battens, are held in place by nails, and when problems appear on these roofs the battens are often found to be the main cause of the trouble (Fig. 8.15). On no account should the size of replacement battens be falsely economic and they should

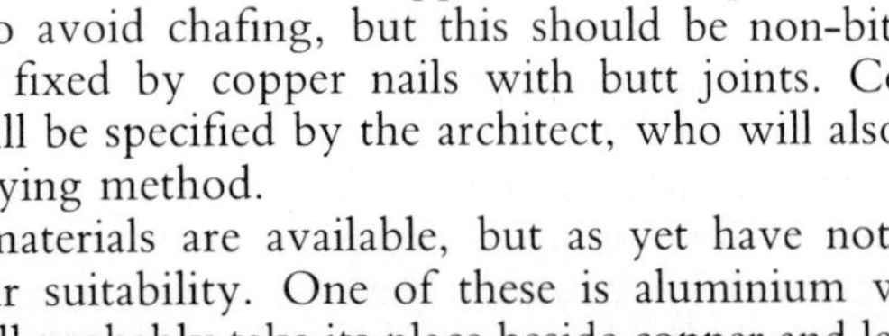

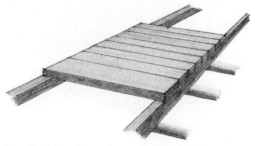

**Fig. 8.16** Duckboards

ɔe fixed very securely to the oak supports by copper nails. If, orig-
nally, the tiles were hung from oak pegs, there is no reason why this ɔractice should not be repeated when they are replaced. If the pitch ɔf the roof is steep it is not necessary to use roofing felt under the ɔattens. At certain intervals it is wise for those responsible for the in- pection of the fabric to move from one part of the roof to another, nd in order to do this duckboards should be provided to give easier ccess to certain parts of the roof and obviate damage to roof cover- ngs (Fig. 8.16). In some places they can be used to contain snow, ɔut they should be properly designed to achieve this and should not ɔlock the channel or gutter they were intended to aid.

# *Chapter 9*
# Bells, bell-frames and belfries

The sound of cathedral and church bells has been one of the distinc tive features of the British way of life. They are not bells fitted onl for chiming, nor are they tubular bells that have no swinging part or carillons; they are the heavy swinging bells which involve th laws of statics and dynamics – heavy pieces of mechanism swingin through almost 360 degrees. Old bells are a real link with the pas and must be attended to with great care, making sure that they ar not defaced in any way. If it is found that they can no longer rin they should be removed – not to be discarded and forgotten but t be preserved within the building where they can be seen and remem bered as pieces of history (Fig. 9.1). One particular defacement th occurs is the removal of the canons (handle-like loops) which, unt the end of the last century, were the means by which the bells wer attached to their headstocks; they also functioned as counter weight It has been the practice to bolt the crown of the bell direct to th headstock. To do this in old bells, an iron staple has to be cast int the bell to support the clapper, and it may be necessary to change th staple periodically as there is a possibility that the bell may fractu due to rust.

When a bell is ringing the clapper can only strike two points of th rim, and if this is allowed to occur over a period of years these poin wear. At some time the clapper's position should be altered to allo it to strike on fresh points; this is known as 'quarter-turning'. If th bell cracks, the tone is spoilt. It is possible to repair a bell by meltin it down and re-using the metal to cast a new bell. A fracture, small, can be repaired by welding, but this will not guarantee a sati factory result as cracks can recur. The delightful sounds that emana from church bells are made of many tones – for example, the 'ta tone', which is the first strike, is followed by the 'hum tone' which

**g. 9.1** (a) elevation

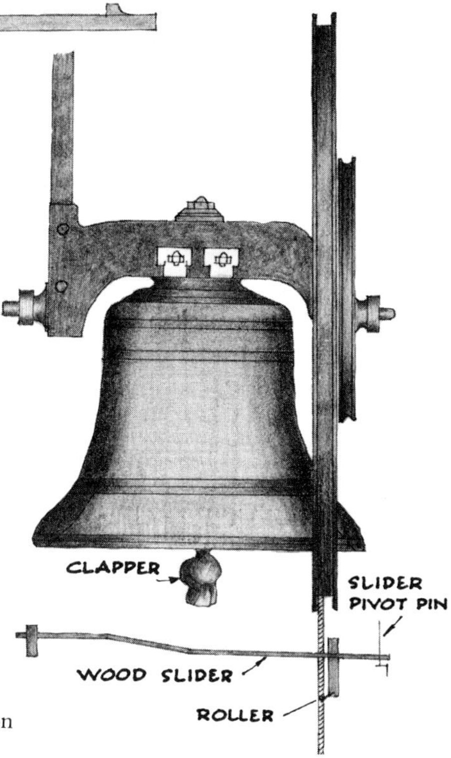


(b) section

a development – and the quality of the sounds depends largely on th blending of the various tones. It has been possible to develop thi aspect, and research has found new ways of adjusting and controllin the tones to produce the most pleasing results. The clapper shoul always strike the centre of the sound-bow otherwise the pin of th clapper joint may be damaged. It should be inspected regularly fo wear, and if any is in evidence the clapper should be re-bushed. It i essential that bells should not be painted, and oil or grease shoul not be used on the sound-bow.

The frame that houses the bells must be strong and rigid becaus the swinging of the bells creates a horizontal force twice the weigh of the bell metal and a vertical force about four times the weight o the bell metal. If the bell-frame is touching the walls of the towe and tends to be springy, certain forces will be set up. It is possibl that the swing of the bells can coincide with the movement in th tower, and this must obviously be watched very closely. It may b necessary to alter the position of the bells or the position of th frame. It is also possible to arrange the bells so that the larger bell cancel the movements of the smaller bells by swinging in the op posite direction.

There are two main types of bell-frame – metal and wood – an each has advantages and disadvantages. In steel and iron frames th nuts and bolts of the fittings and framework require regular tighten ing. This procedure is most important when the headstock i wooden and must be done evenly all round, otherwise the bell wi be thrown out of alignment. The bolt passes through the bell at th centre and must always be tight. When this bolt is being tightene the split-pin must be removed and replaced. Timber bell-frames wi require as close attention as the other woodwork considered i Chapter 7. As in steel and iron frames, the bolts must always be tigl and the beams that support the bell-frames should be free from deca and beetle attack, especially at the beam ends. One of the first sign that a fault may be present is movement of the bell-frame during th ringing of the bells, and this is a serious matter. A great deal of ca is necessary when lubricating the machinery; for example, the hou ing of the main ball-bearings need only be lubricated after long inte vals of ten to twelve years, unless otherwise recommended by th bell foundry. The bearing caps, which are secured by four screw must not be removed. If the old type of bearings exist they shou not be allowed to become too worn, and it would be wise to lubrica bearings of this type each time the bells are rung. To ensure that th wooden sliders are in an efficient condition and are functioning pro erly, an application of black lead should be given to the tips of th sliders and runners. The sliders must be treated with grease.

The durability of steel and iron frames depends, to a great exter on repainting at regular intervals; and wooden frames will rema sound if they are given proper attention. Bell-ropes are subjected an enormous amount of wear and should be repositioned frequently o prevent chafing where they pass through the 'garter hole' in the wheel. There will be friction on the ropes at this point and also where they pass through the guides; wear and tear can be reduced by rubbing tallow on the ropes. The ropes must be constantly inspected for signs of fraying. Fraying can be caused, for example, by a screw working loose in a guide or thimble through the ceiling, and all screws must therefore be secured before any attempt is made to attach a new rope or to splice the old. In the bell-tower there are usually louvres, or shutters which are tongued and grooved to give ventilation and to allow the egress of sound. It is important to prevent the entrance of birds, and all louvres should therefore be covered internally with copper wire screens.

When giving consideration to the structure of the bell-tower, it has o be decided if the bell-frame is in the best position – an assessment hat will include the acoustic properties. It is important to hear the bells to advantage externally, and every effort must be made to achieve this. The internal acoustic properties of the structure are also mportant. The peal inside the building must not be a deafening experience intruding on pre-worship meditation, but it should still be audible in the ringing chamber. To achieve this there should be two loors between the belfry and the chamber, and the upper floor, the deafening chamber', must be independent of the beams which carry he bell-frame.

If a bell-tower shows signs of weakness it can be strengthened for bell-ringing. Vibration is bound to occur, but it can be contained. It s essential that the tower should act as a structural unity and not be a onflict of sections working against each other. If it is thought that tructural attention is necessary, it can include the insertion of stitches at different levels or replacement of the timber roof by a reinforced concrete slab (Fig. 9.2).

The beams which support the bell-frame must be strong enough

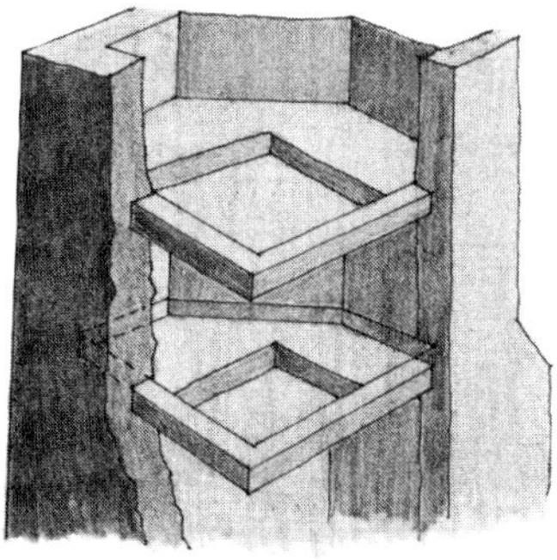

**Fig. 9.2** Stitches at different levels

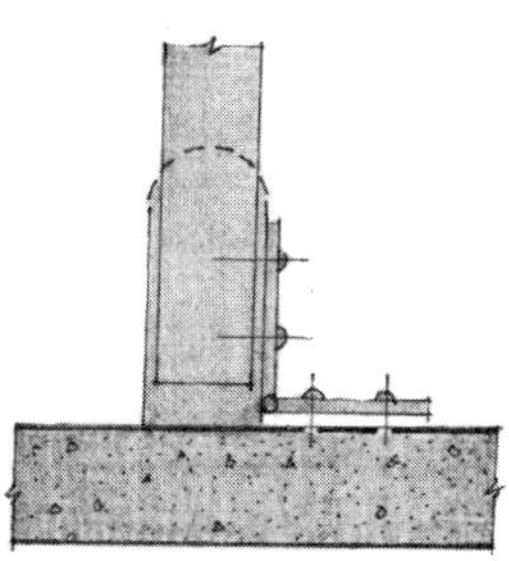

**Fig. 9.3** Flagpole swivel-bottom

to be rigid in themselves and should be firmly held in a rigid state between the surrounding walls. This prevents each beam acting as a battering ram to its adjacent walls. If necessary, these beams can be combined with a reinforced concrete girdle around the tower. The tower can also have cross-beams in the opposite direction to create, in effect, a grid-iron which holds the tower together at this level.

If a tower contains a clock, the oil should be removed and the mechanism cleaned and lubricated every three months, with each part having clean oil applied. If there are signs of damage or wear, or if the pulley wheels are cracking or rusting, then these – together with the suspension rings, striking mechanism and wire ropes – should be referred to the manufacturers or to someone who has experience of this kind of mechanism. A clock is a feature of many towers and its maintenance is important not just as a time-piece but because it can deteriorate and effect the tower structure. A flag-pole is also a feature of many towers, but can be a source of danger when fixed by metal fastenings as they may rust and crack the stone. The continued movement of the flag-pole by the elements, and the billowing of the flag, can make it unsafe. There is the added hazard of water entering the pole causing it to rot at the point where it is joined to its support. A lightning conductor should be fitted, but if it is ineffective it becomes a serious danger. The conductor must be tested every year to ensure that the earthing resistance does not exceed 10 ohms. There have been recommendations that no new flag-poles should be erected on bell-towers, and it is even suggested that where they exist they should be removed. They are best erected in a convenient position on the ground and fitted with a swivel-bottom which allows them to be lowered for easy maintenance (Fig. 9.3).

# *Chapter 10*
# Materials and services

The previous chapters have dealt with the major structural parts of cathedral and church architecture, but there remain a number of aspects of the fabric that require a good deal of attention as they form integral parts of a medieval building. For convenience they will be considered in alphabetical order.

## Acoustics

Briefly, acoustics can be defined as the origin, propagation and auditory sensation of sound. Some general principles are referred to, but the main requirement is a satisfactory level that is sufficiently loud without distortion (Fig. 10.1).

In the case of ecclesiastical buildings we are thinking particularly of the architectural use of space and materials and in the control of voice and instruments in order that they can be heard to their best advantage. Scientifically this is known as the 'optimum reverberation time', and this will vary according to the type of music played.

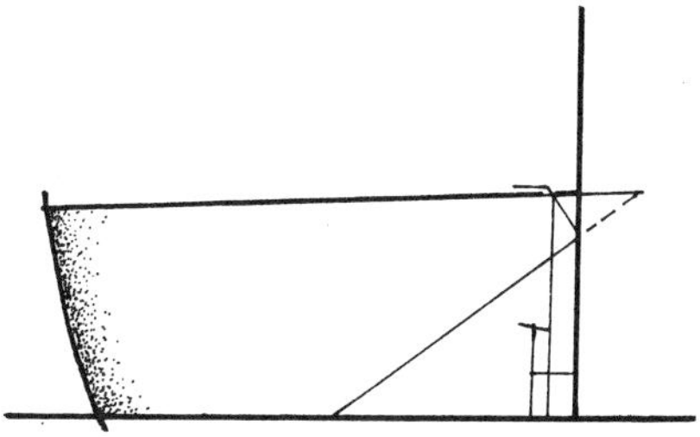

**Fig. 10.1** Acoustics

There has been a substantial development in the music used within the church building, and linked with this is the use of sophisticated sound relaying systems.

Some basic principles apply. We must first consider echo, which more or less follows the same geometrical rules as light – that is, it is reflected by a hard surface in the same way that light is reflected by a mirror. Sound that is reflected has to travel further than sound that goes directly from singer or speaker to listener. An important difference is that sound travels considerably slower than light, and the delay produces an echo. Then we must consider reverberation – a situation in which the waves of sound jump and bounce in all directions depending on the type of obstacles, such as pillars, vaults, pews and chairs. This creates a background noise which develops and continues after the original sound has died. Choral music has been so composed that this is allowed for, but that does not automatically mean that speech is satisfactory. In the case of the echo, a basic remedy is to change the shape of the reflecting surface, which is not easy in an old building, or to cover the surface with an absorbent material. Reverberation can be controlled by the use of soft materials which absorb the sound waves, a fact which becomes apparent if we compare an empty church building with one that has the presence of a congregation. Clarity is obtained when there is the absence of overlapping of successive sounds, and an optimum reverberation period is achieved. Reverberation need only be sufficient to obtain the fullness of tone.

The application of these principles, and any remedial action that may be thought necessary, can be limited when giving respect to tradition and antiquity. The important thing is that the preacher must be heard, and the voice must be reinforced if it has to travel into 'empty' areas before being reflected to the places at which it is intended to be heard. The size of the building will be considered; its acoustic qualities will be examined; and this will be defined in the use of the building. Solution of this problem must be under the direction of those who specialise in acoustics, and it is essential that they supervise the entire work, both to preserve the fabric and its fittings and to achieve the best sound.

## Decoration

At first, and in comparison with other buildings, this may not appear to be a major item in the care and preservation of cathedrals and churches. In the ecclesiastical sense it requires careful and sensitive attention and probably the main consideration is the treatment of the woodwork. In this context the word 'decoration' is used in its artistic, practical sense. Oak ages to a beautiful colour, as can be seen by the many example in old pews and screens. Internal woodwork n the first hundred years of its life, turns a raw colour if it is not :reated. In some cases wax has been applied, with good intention, to preserve it but this has created an unpleasant tone. Ammonia has been used with disastrous results: at first it appears to be satisfactory, but the red flush that follows destroys the beauty that is intrinsic in he wood.

Internally and externally, medieval cathedrals and churches were, at one time, very colourful buildings. Over the centuries the colours have faded and most of them have disappeared although the author has seen parts of such buildings sensitively restored. This kind of work demands advice from an expert as it is essential to obtain balance and contrast in the placing of colours.

## Distemper and internal plasterwork

t is possible to apply a lime-wash to the stonework of internal walls. The rough rubble walls which were intended to have a thin coating of plaster have, in many cases, been stripped during the last century. This has proved to be quite fortuitous as it has exposed some very nteresting rubble work. It may be wise to re-plaster in some intances, in which case a lime-wash applied to the wall can give the ight colour to the texture required. Such an application is unwise on shlar quoins; nor is lime-wash treatment appropriate for external wall faces.

If it is necessary to re-plaster a wall it must be remembered that listemper does not adhere well to new plaster, and if the distemper is oloured it is likely to fade in patches. Any necessary distempering hould be postponed until at least six months after plastering has een completed. If the distemper has to be applied immediately it is wise to make certain that the correct liquid is used, and in this respect expert advice should be obtained.

Reference must be made to the condition of old plaster becoming ilapidated. We must also draw attention to the possibility of nedieval wall paintings being hidden, as successive layers of plaster an hide the most historic and exquisite murals. Should any discovery be made, no further work should proceed until expert advice as been obtained. The guidance needed is far beyond the scope of his book.

The risks of stripping plaster internally are not as great inside the uilding as outside. It would seem that in the past people impulsively tripped plaster from rubble walls which were not intended to be are in the first place.

Ceilings that become defective can be satisfactorily renewed by roprietary wallboards, which in any case may be preferred to lath nd plaster as it is a much cheaper method. They also have the dvantage of providing heat insulation and are not greatly affected by vibration. Wallboards are a 'modern' introduction to interior work, and are neat and tidy; however, they may not offer the most appealing aesthetic solution in medieval building.

## Heating

This can be a heavy item of expenditure and requires careful assessment. The heat requirement can vary from one building to another depending on the system installed and the condition of the fabric. Ir numerous cases the existing or original system had become an eyesore and was so inefficient that it had to be replaced. In most cathedrals and many churches a satisfactory scheme has been workec out, but if a system of heating is still under consideration it will b wise to investigate alternative schemes before reaching any decision It seems sensible to relate the system to where heat is most required – that is, where people are gathered – but it also should be adequate t provide a temperature that gives the right atmosphere throughou the fabric, although this may depend to some extent on financia resources.

Electrical systems are probably more inconspicuous in cathedral and churches. If an electrical system is not feasible, a new heatin chamber may be necessary. This is not just an aesthetic problem, a fumes have to be considered which can be objectionable to peopl and damaging to the fabric. If some buildings do have to use othe methods of heating, careful examination of the flues must be made This will be essential if a new and different method of heating i installed, for inefficient or inappropriate flues can cause considerabl expenditure.

We have inherited from the nineteenth century floor ducts whic are covered with gratings (Fig. 10.2) An attempt has been made t

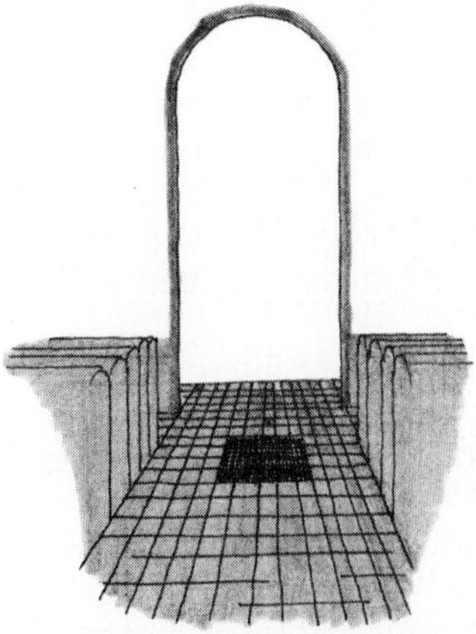

**Fig. 10.2** Grating

replace them, but they still exist in many churches and have to be maintained. It is best not to renew such systems, even if it is being considered, as they become constant dirt traps. The object of one hot-water heating system in an ecclesiastical building is to warm the walls and external windows, with the intention of preventing down-draughts. One of the constant problems that exists, however, is the complaint from worshippers that even when every door and window is closed there is a persistent downdrought. This is caused by air cooling quickly as it makes contact with windows and walls, and then falling on the congregation. The same principle applies here as in other cases: a specialist will be needed for advice and to carry out any new heating installation.

## Lighting

This section will be brief, not because it is less important, but because it is a specialist subject. Electricity is the most convenient form of lighting but it requires skill and knowledge in order to comply with all the safety regulations – which are extremely stringent, with particular emphasis on the fire hazard. So many electrical installations in cathedrals and churches are neglected for years (the kind of neglect that would not be tolerated anywhere else), with inevitable breakdown and failure. In this particular service, the method of installation must be carefully directed. Without care and attention it can so easily end up decorating the fabric with cables and conduits perched on ledges and lodged in the fluting or moulding in an attempt to disguise the new work and cover up any poor workmanship. Lighting has been developed to a very advanced and sophisticated standard of design, and each cathedral and church will have to decide which is best for its particular requirements.

## Brickwork

The bricks that were used in the medieval period were irregular in shape and tended to be rough in texture (Fig. 10.3). It was the practice to lay the bricks in shallow courses with thick joints of lime mortar. In dealing with this kind of old brickwork it is necessary to keep the mortar more porous than the bricks. Before attempting to attend to these bricks, care must be given to the removal of every kind of vegetation and roots. If it is difficult to obtain suitable matching bricks, it will be possible to re-use those from the inside of a wall on the face of a new wall. When re-pointing is involved, the walls should be saturated with water and the joints should be raked out to a depth of at least ¾ in. (20 mm). The walls should be pointed with a fairly dry mix.

**Fig. 10.3** Medieval brickwork

## Metalwork

Some of the most attractive features of cathedrals and churches are i the form of wrought ironwork (Fig. 10.4), which can rust and scal very easily if neglected. Paint that is flaking can be removed by stripping agent, after which the ironwork needs to be completel rubbed down and treated with a rust remover. There will be th temptation to replace apparently old sections with new, but thi must be resisted as much as possible otherwise it can become a ver patchy feature. It is much better to preserve the original.

The attention that needs to be given to wrought iron is not usuall a complicated process, and with a good blacksmith shop is easil undertaken. Most of the work required is in strengthening join which may need welding or in straightening bent members. If th metalwork has to be removed from its permanent position, it shoul be protected by rust-inhibiting paint before re-fixing. Certain fe tures – for example, the ends of railings built into the stonework can be tipped with bronze or have a copper sleeve in an attempt t overcome the possibility of rust. Gates, hinge-pins and other fitting should be cleaned regularly, and special attention should be given t medieval furniture, where the key-plate and hinges provide historic interest.

**Fig. 10.4** Wrought ironwork

## Rainwater furniture

Neglected cast-iron gutters and downpipes can be the source of serious problems (Fig. 10.5). Medieval cathedrals and churches are often fortunate enough to have projecting eaves, as well as gargoyles (Fig. 1.10) and spouts, which are quite adequate to deal with the discharge of rainwater. If this is the case it may be unwise to introduce

**Fig. 10.5** Cast-iron gutters and downpipes

gutters and downpipes as they can become a hindrance rather than a help. Where they do exist, it is essential to be meticulous in their maintenance. They are usually made of cast-iron lead. In the case of cast-iron furniture, rust will be the greatest hazard and is usually due to a lack of painting. Painting does not have to be ignored to cause problems; it can be skimped, especially if the downpipes are too close to the face of the wall in which case they should be refixed with projecting lugs to allow regular painting of the complete unit with bituminous paints.

If it is fixed correctly, lead has a long lifespan and also allows for thermal movement. It requires continuous support to avoid any kind of sag or slope, and vertical downpipes are usually fixed by lead 'ears'. Where the medieval building is fortunate enough to have its original lead furniture, it should be retained as it is an architectural feature of some merit and value, probably seen best of all in rain-water heads. Plastic guttering and piping are available and are manufactured to a high standard. If they are grey, they are aesthetically acceptable. They do not require much maintenance and are better unpainted on ecclesiastical buildings of the medieval period.

# *Epilogue*

William Morris once said 'Stave off decay by daily care', and probably no one has ever given better advice concerning the care and preservation of medieval cathedrals and churches. By their nature they are vulnerable through age, materials and artistic value, and therefore require very sensitive treatment.

Various terms have been used to indicate the type of maintenance these buildings require – repair, restoration, conservation, preservation – and each of these terms has a particular meaning.

'Repair' usually means to mend something, but this, in itself, may not be sufficient and must be considered in the context of one or more of the other aspects. If 'restoration' is required, does this mean that the building is to be restored to its original condition? Not necessarily. Also, the cases for 'conservation' and 'preservation' can be considered separately or together. This, however, is not the place to introduce a philosophical argument. We have considered and used the word 'preservation' in the widest sense because of our care and concern for these buildings. Each word has its place in relation to cathedrals and churches; in some cases the most appropriate action will be repair, at other times it will be restoration, and at all times we must consider conservation and preservation. It does not really matter which word we use. In the end they all mean 'care', which is an on-going thing and continues forever.

Our cathedrals and churches are a vital part of our heritage; they are in the main important pieces of architecture and in one way or another contain something of value which is an asset that we cannot afford to lose.

# Glossary

**Abacus**: The uppermost member of a capital.
**Aisle**: Originally a projection from the side wall of a building; now a lateral addition separated from the main structure by an arcade or row of posts.
**Annulet**: A ring round a circular pier or shaft.
**Apse**: The semi-circular or polygonal end to a building.
**Arcade**: A row of arches.
**Arch**: A structure of wedge-shaped blocks which, over an opening, support one another by mutual pressure.
**Ashlaring**: Timber struts forming a wall or partition; the vertical frame forming the side walls of an attic storey.
**Ashlar**: Hewn and squared struts prepared for building.
**Ball flower**: A form of ornament, consisting of globular three-petalled flowers enclosing small balls.
**Banker**: The stone bench upon which the masons work.
**Batter**: The slope of a wall backwards from the vertical.
**Barrel vault**: A stone arched roof, as in a tunnel.
**Bay**: The transverse division of a building where bays are marked by vaulting shafts or pillars.
**Billett**: a short roll at intervals in hollow moulding.
**Bond**: A method of arranging vertical joints in masonry so that no two appear immediately above each other.
**Boss**: In ribbed vaulting, an ornamental projection to conceal the intersection of the ribs.
**Box gutter**: A lead gutter provided behind the parapet to collect water falling upon the roof.
**Brace**: A diagonal stiffener in woodwork.
**Broach**: A medieval term for a spire.
**Buttress**: A masonry support against overturning pressure upon a wall.
**Cat-beam**: Timber passing longitudinally beneath the collars of a late medieval roof, and carried by the king post.
**Centring**: A temporary wooden paving upon which an arch is turned.
**Chain**: An ornamental stitch.
**Chancel**: The eastern arm of a church.
**Chapter house**: The place of

assembly of the dean and canons for cathedral business.
**Chevron**: A zig-zag form of ornamentation of the Norman period.
**Choir**: A portion of a great church, in which those serving it sing the offices.
**Claw**: A bolster with a serrated edge, used for smoothing axed stonework before tooling.
**Clerestory**: The portion of a building raised above certain structures to provide sites for windows to light its interior.
**Cloister**: A covered walk usually walled on one side and open on to a court or quadrangle on the other, especially of a religious building.
**Close**: The enclosed precinct of a cathedral church.
**Collar**: A short horizontal timber tying a pair or 'couple' of rafters near the apex.
**Column**: A stone support, either monolithic or, more usually, built in drums.
**Corbel table**: A feature of the eaves, consisting of a miniature arcade carried by corbels.
**Core**: The hollow of a masonry wall; it is filled with a 'spalls' and mortar as the work proceeds.
**Cornice**: Projecting eave, which is moulded.
**Couple**: A pair of rafters pegged together at the apex of the roof.
**Course**: A layer of stones in masonry.
**Crocket**: A projecting block of stone carved in Gothic foliage on the inclined sides of pinnacles and canopies.
**Crossing**: The area beneath the central tower of a church.
**Cross vault**: Intersecting barrel vaults.
**Cross wall**: A stone partition.
**Cruciform**: A church in which all four arms are of the same span as the crossing.
**Cruck**: A pair of heavy inclined beams supporting longitudinal roof; timbers.
**Crypt**: A space beneath the main floor of a church; a vaulted lower storey
**Crypto-cruciform**: Relating to a church having a central tower flanked by narrower wings or transepts.
**Cubiform capital**: A cushion capital with angles cut off and turned sideways to reduce the projection of the abacus.
**Cushion capital**: A Byzantine version of the Doric capital, having that portion of the capital joining an abacus to a shaft, pillar or column square on plan.
**Cusp**: A point separating foliation in Gothic tracery.
**Diaper**: Reticulated decorative work.
**Disc**: Thin, flat, circular moulding used around doorways in 12th century.
**Drag**: A serrated scraper used for obliterating tool marks on masonry.
**Dripstone**: A moulding over the heads of doorways, windows and archways to throw off the rain.
**Drum**: A masonry course, in a pillar or a column, formed by single stones.
**Duplex bay**: The bay of a great church having a pillar or column set between two piers.
**Eaves**: The projecting part of a roof.
**Fan vault**: A late medieval vault in which the ribs and web are combined to form a style of ornament resembling open fans.
**Fillet**: A narrow, flat band which divides mouldings from one another; also separates column flutes.
**Finial**: An ornament finishing off the apex of a roof, gable, pediment, pinnacle, newel, canopy, etc.
**Flushwork**: A wall decoration

formed by stone panelling filled with knapped flintwork.
**Flying arch**: An arch spanning a building, as in the case of the transverse rib of a vault, or carrying longitudinal flooring or roof timbers.
**Flying buttress**: A flying arch, or a system of these, carrying the thrust of a roof or vault towards an isolated buttress.
**Foil**: The spaces between cusps in Gothic tracery; trefoil, quatrefoil, etc., indicate the number of foils in the window light.
**Foliated**: Silhouette divided by 'cusps' into foils, each of which is the segment of a circle.
**Form**: See 'template'.
**Four poster**: Byzantine or Byzantinesque church having a central feature carried upon four supports and surrounded by equal projections on all four sides.
**Frame**: The timber frame upon which later medieval buildings were constructed.
**Freestone**: Stone capable of being worked by a mason.
**Gable**: The wall filling the end of a roof.
**Gargoyle**: A decorated stone spout carrying water from a box gutter through the parapet.
**Girder**: A beam tying the opposite walls of a frame structure.
**Groin**: The line of intersection between two portions of a cross vault.
**Groined vault**: A cross vault having no vaulting ribs.
**Hammer-beam**: A short length of tie-beam, supported on a wooden spandrel, rising from a corbel or another hammer-beam.
**Head**: The upper horizontal member of an opening or frame.
**Hood mould**: Moulding provided above an arch to prevent water streaming down the wall face.
**Impost**: The springing line of an arch.
**Impost moulding**: Moulding indicating impost.
**Jamb**: The side of an opening.
**Joist**: A small beam, carrying floor.
**King-post**: A short post set upon a tie-beam and carrying a cat-beam.
**Lady chapel**: A chapel dedicated to the Virgin, east of the high altar.
**Lantern**: A structure for ventilation and light; takes the form of a tower in Gothic architecture.
**Lights**: The principle divisions of a window.
**Lintel**: A timber or stone beam spanning an opening.
**Louvre**: A ventilation consisting of horizontal sloping slats allowing the passage of air but excluding rain; often used to keep birds out of towers.
**Masonry**: Dressed stonework laid in courses.
**Misericord**: A bracket on the underside of a hinged wooden seat in a choir stall.
**Mortar**: The matrix in which masonry is set.
**Mullion**: The vertical structural member subdividing a window.
**Nave**: The western limb of a cathedral, for congregation.
**Niche**: A recess in a wall hollowed out to receive sculpture.
**Ogee**: A moulding incorporating a convex and concave curve.
**Order**: A single ring of voussoirs forming part of a complete arch.
**Pan**: The principle beam carried upon posts.
**Parapet**: A light, protective wall.
**Parvise (Paradise)**: The space before the west door of a great church, council chamber or episcopal palace; the room above a church porch.
**Pier**: A support in masonry; resembling a portion of wall retained to carry an arch or beam.
**Pilaster**: A vertical strip, often fashioned to imitate a column.
**Pillar**: A free-standing vertical support.

**Pinnacle**: The masonry employed as a weight at the summit of buttress or in decorative form as a finial.
**Piscina**: The stone basin provided in walling next to the altar for washing holy vessels.
**Pitch**: The inclination of a roof from the horizontal.
**Plaster**: Mortar employed to cover the walls or ceilings.
**Plate**: A horizontal timber set upon a wall-top to carry the feet of rafters.
**Plate tracery**: Thirteenth century triforium designed windows.
**Plinth**: The base of a masonry structure.
**Pole**: A medieval unit of measurement, about 16 ft (4.8 m) in length.
**Poppy-head**: A finial used to decorate the tops of benches of stall end.
**Porch**: A structure covering an external door.
**Presbytery**: The eastern termination of the choir.
**Pseudo-cruciform**: Relating to a church with wings or transepts, but no central tower.
**Pulpitum**: An elaborate structure forming a screen at the entrance to the choir of a late medieval great church.
**Purlin**: A longitudinal timber passing between trusses and helping to support rafters.
**Quatrefoil**: A four-lobed ornamental infilling for a circle or arch head.
**Quadripartite vault**: A vault supported by a pair of diagonal ribs only.
**Quarry**: A small diamond-shaped pane used in medieval glazing.
**Quoin**: A corner stone.
**Rafter**: A sloping timber in pitched roof construction.
**Relieving arch**: An arch turned in the walling above an arch or a lintel to relieve pressure.
**Reredos**: The architectural background to an altar.
**Respond**: A half-pillar terminating an arcade.
**Reticulated tracery**: Tracery of net-like character, single pattern, consisting of circles drawn out at the top and bottom in ogee-shaped points and repeated over a whole area.
**Reveal**: A masonry lining to a door or window opening.
**Rib**: A light, skeleton arch carrying vaulting.
**Ridge**: A spine or summit or a pitched roof with longitudinal timber.
**Romanesque**: A style of architecture prevalent in western Europe from about the ninth to twelfth centuries.
**Rood**: A crucifix.
**Rood beam**: A beam-supporting partition filling the upper portion of a chancel arch and forming the background to a rood.
**Rood loft**: A projecting gallery provided before a rood.
**Rood screen**: A chancel screen.
**Rood stair**: A stair to the rood loft.
**Rubble**: Unwrought stone.
**Saddle-bar**: A horizontal bar reinforcing lead glazing.
**Sanctuary**: The area within the chancel rails.
**Sedilia**: Stone seats formed in the wall of the sanctuary.
**Severy**: A portion of the vault web enclosed between a series of ribs.
**Sexpartite vault**: A vault which has an additional transverse rib crossing each bay.
**Shaft**: A slender column.
**Soffit**: The underside of an arch or lintel.
**Spall** A flake chipped from stone.
**Spandrel**: An approximately triangular area in elevation.
**Springing**: Supporting stone from which arch is formed.
**Squinch**: An arch constructed across an internal angle. A small arch running diagonally across the corner of a square tower or room; it

supports a side of an octagonal tower or spire.
**Stanchion**: A vertical bar in a window light. An arch across the angle of a square tower to carry the side of an octagon.
**Steeple**: A staged construction surmounting a tower.
**String**: A moulding or projecting course set horizontally along the elevation of a building.
**String course**: Horizontal moulding used for punctuation.
**Tablet or Table**: A medieval term applied to all horizontal bands of moulding.
**Tail**: In masonry, the portion of the stone concealed within the wall.
**Template**: The full size of a moulding; used by a mason when cutting stones.
**Tie-beam**: A beam used for tying across wall plates that may spread outwards under pressure from the roof.
**Tierceron ribs**: Pairs of ribs, with the same point of springing as principal ribs, meeting obliquely instead of being carried across from one side of a vault to the other in a continuous line.
**Toothing stone**: A stone left projecting at end of wall at alternate courses.
**Tracery**: The pattern of stone bars at the head of a window; also used for ornamenting wall surface.
**Transept**: The transverse arm of a cruciform church.
**Transom**: A horizontal structure member subdividing a window.
**Triforium**: The passage to the clerestory of a large church.
**Turret**: A small tower; often a staircase.
**Tympanum**: The semi-circular space between a lintel and its relieving arch.
**Vault**: An arched covering in stone, brick or wood.
**Voussoir**: An arch stone.
**Web**: Stone filling of vault between ribs.

# Index